DISCARDED

THE STORY OF
NEW AMSTERDAM

PETER STUYVESANT

*From the original painting in the possession
of the New York Historical Society*

THE
STORY
OF
NEW AMSTERDAM

BY WILLIAM R. SHEPHERD
Columbia University

Ira J. Friedman Division
KENNIKAT PRESS
Port Washington, N.Y.

THE STORY OF NEW AMSTERDAM

First published in 1926
Reissued in 1970 by Ira J. Friedman, Inc.
Library of Congress Catalog Card No: 75-118790
ISBN 0-87198-088-6
Manufactured in the United States of America

EMPIRE STATE HISTORICAL PUBLICATIONS SERIES No. 88

TO
T. S.

FOREWORD

The year 1926 marks the three hundredth anniversary of the founding of the tiny Dutch trading-post that was to become the metropolis of America. It commemorates also what has been called the greatest transaction in real estate ever made on Manhattan—or elsewhere. Purchase from the aboriginal folk who roamed over the site of the future city gave at least a color of title to the emigrants from overseas who were to establish on it a new home. However small the depletion of their purses, their consciences assuredly were far lighter as they set out upon the task of planting civilization in the wilderness.

Then and there began the process that was to transform a quaint little settlement of Netherlanders perched on the southern tip of Manhattan into the huge cosmopolitan city of the present. The mind that runs back through the intervening centuries to observe its origins conjures up a vision of achievement more wondrous indeed than the tales of Arabian magic.

Foreword

For the founders themselves to have imagined the outcome of their handiwork required a gift of prophecy which they could not possess. The generation of to-day, privileged to survey the result as well as to view its struggling inception, must ever regret that the pioneers were denied a share in the contemplation of what was to be accomplished. As we invoke the shades of a distant past, therefore, let us call up in memory the townsmen of the time when Old New York was young New Amsterdam, and bid them rejoice with us in spirit that they builded so wisely and so well!

The following sketch that seeks to tell of their deeds is reprinted with certain changes from the copyright Year-book for 1917 of The Holland Society of New York. For courteous permission to reissue it in this form the author expresses his thanks to Mr. Tunis G. Bergen, Chairman of the Society's Committee on History and Tradition. In preparing the new edition he appreciates the friendly aid received from Mr. Victor H. Paltsits, of the New York Public Library, to whose expert knowledge students of the period are under deep obligation.

W. R. S.

CONTENTS

CHAPTER I
THE TRADING-POST　　　3

CHAPTER II
THE VILLAGE　　　23

CHAPTER III
THE TOWN　　　63

CHAPTER IV
THE MUNICIPALITY　　　105

CHAPTER V
THE CITY-TO-BE　　　133

CHAPTER VI
THE PASSING OF NEW AMSTERDAM　　　170

ILLUSTRATIONS

Peter Stuyvesant *Frontispiece*
From the original painting in the possession of the New York Historical Society

Section of "Adriaen Block map," 1614, showing New Netherland 5
Documents relative to the colonial history of the state of New York, I.

Title-page of the edict of the States General of the Netherlands, concerning the establishment of a West India Company, 1621 8
Courtesy of the New York Public Library

Title-page of the charter granted to the West India Company, June 3, 1621 8
Courtesy of the New York Public Library

[xi]

Illustrations

Portion of a letter written at Amsterdam, November 5, 1626, announcing the purchase of the "island Manhattes from the wild men for the value of sixty guilders"   11
  From a facsimile in the New York Public Library of the original in the Rijks Archief at The Hague

Portion of the earliest extant original letter written in New Amsterdam. Jonas Michaelius to Joannes Foreest, August 8, 1628   15
  From Manhattan in 1628 Edited by Dingman Versteeg

Title-page of the "Privileges and Exemptions" granted by the West India Company, June 7, 1629, for the encouragement of colonization in New Netherland   42
  Courtesy of the New York Public Library

Section of the "Visscher map" of New Netherland, 1655, with a view of New Amsterdam   62
  Adriaen vander Donck, Beschrijvinge van Nieuw Nederlandt. Amsterdam, 1656

Illustrations

Section of map, 1630, showing New Netherland and its neighbor, New England 83
Joannes de Laet, Nieuwe Wereldt, ofte Beschrijvinghe van West Indien, Leyden, 1630

First page of the oldest extant records of the court of burgomasters and schepens of New Amsterdam, February 6, 1653 98
From a Fascimile in the New York Public Library

The seal of New Amsterdam 121
Courtesy of the New York Historical Society

Section of map, 1679, showing New Amsterdam along the East River from the fort to the town hall 155
"Journal of Jasper Danskaerts," Long Island Historical Society Memoirs, I.

Cornelius Steenwijck, sometime schepen of New Amsterdam, and mayor of New York, 1668–1670. Note the view of New Amsterdam below 163
From the original painting in the possession of the New York Historical Society

Illustrations

View of New York, late New Amsterdam,
1670   188
*Arnoldus Montanus, De Nieuwe en
Onbekende Weereld, of Beschrijving
van America. Amsterdam, 1671*

The last resting-place of Peter Stuyvesant 192
*From a photograph in the possession
of the New York Historical Society*

Signatures of Dutch governors—Peter Minuit, Wouter van Twiller, William Kieft, Peter Stuyvesant and Anthony Colve   199

THE STORY OF
NEW AMSTERDAM

CHAPTER I

THE TRADING-POST

THE seventeenth century was peculiarly the age of great commercial companies, organized for trade and colonization, endowed by their governments with extensive powers, and given a monopoly in their various transactions. Of these corporations the Dutch East India Company was a notable example. A few years after its foundation it entrusted to Henry Hudson, an English sailor who had done good service in Arctic waters, the task of finding a northwest passage to Asia, which would lessen the long journey around the Cape of Good Hope, or through the Straits of Magellan.

Though French and Spanish navigators may have seen the mouth of the river that was to bear the name of Hudson, eighty years and more before September 12, 1609, when the "Half Moon" cautiously poked its nose into the lower

The Story *of* New Amsterdam

bay, the real credit for its discovery belongs to the Anglo-Dutch captain. It was his achievement that made the stream known to the European world and rendered it commercially useful. Here local legend affirms the sober truth of history, for when it thunders in the Catskills the children and the old people say that Hendrik Hudson and his phantom crew are playing at skittles. Could Hudson have peered through the mist of the coming centuries and have caught a vision of the mighty city on Manhattan for whose Dutch foundation he had himself provided, the thought of seeking a northwest passage to India must have seemed a trivial thing.

Though variously derived and interpreted, the commonly accepted meaning of the Indian word from which the name "Manhattan" was taken is "island of the hills." In the seventeenth century its southern part showed a series of wooded hills, some of them eighty feet above the present street level, interspersed with grassy valleys, a chain of swamps and a deep pond. To the northward lay high and rocky ground rising at times to 240 feet above tide-water.

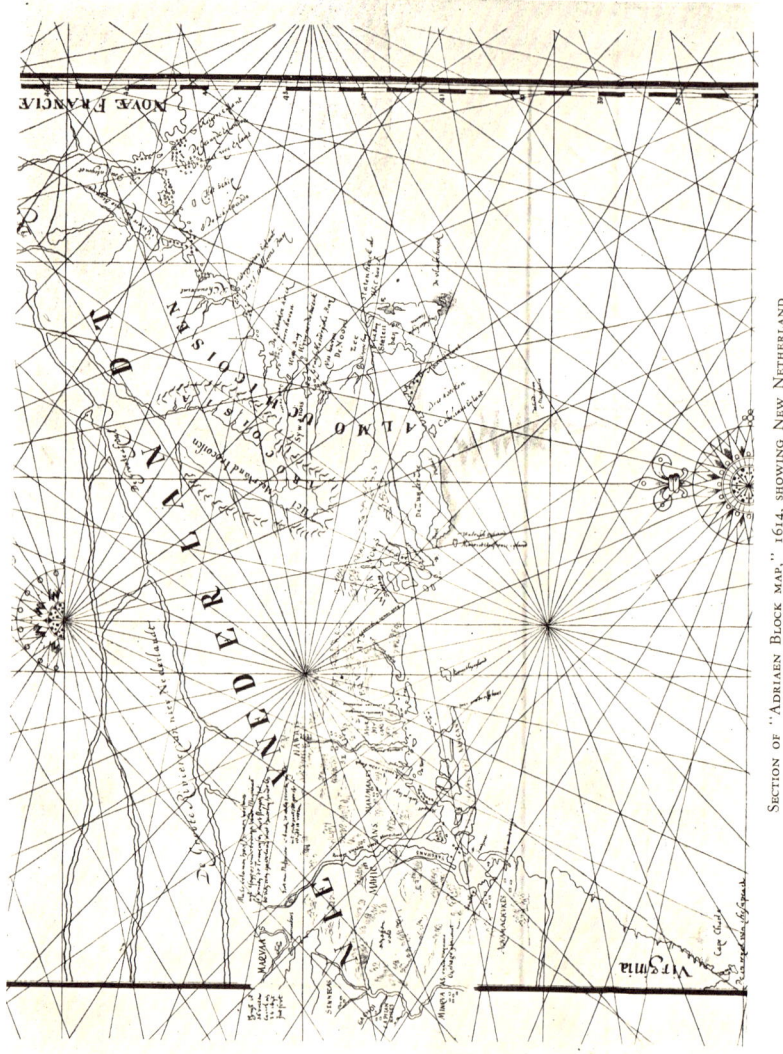

Section of "Adriaen Block Map," 1614, showing New Netherland

Documents relative to the colonial history of the State of New York, i.

The Trading-Post

While it is true that the Dutch East India Company, interested only in Asiatic commerce, saw fit to ignore Hudson's report on the possibilities of the fur-trade in the region that he had visited, in 1614 certain merchants of Amsterdam procured from the government of the Netherlands a grant that would enable them to turn such advantages to good account. In the language of the grant, "whereas we understand it would be honorable, serviceable and profitable to this country, and for the promotion of its prosperity, as well as for the maintenance of seafaring people, that the good inhabitants should be excited and encouraged to employ and occupy themselves in seeking out and discovering passages, havens, countries and places . . . and being informed by some traders that they intended with God's merciful help, by diligence, labor, danger and expense, to employ themselves thereat, as they expect to derive a handsome profit therefrom," a monopoly of trade between the fortieth and the forty-fifth parallels of latitude, i. e. between Virginia and New France, was to be guaranteed for a specified period. The body organized for the pur-

The Story *of* New Amsterdam

pose had no powers of government, but merely the rights of discovery and trade, the latter of which, apparently, was prosecuted with some vigor during the allotted term.

The initiative to actual settlement came with the incorporation, in 1621, of the Dutch West India Company, a New World counterpart of the Dutch East India Company. This body was vested with extraordinary and almost exclusive authority for twenty-four years, subject to renewal, over the "barbarous coasts" of Africa and America. The government of the Netherlands reserved the right of supervision, regulation and appeal in specific cases. The management of the corporation, with its five distinct city chambers or boards, was entrusted to a Council of Nineteen; but the ordinary direction of affairs in North America fell to the Amsterdam Chamber alone.

The terms of the charter granted to the Dutch West India Company will bear a brief inspection, for they show that the operations in "New Netherland"—the name now definitely attached to the Hudson region—concerned only a business venture. According to the charter,

The Trading-Post

the director general, or "governor" as the English called him, of New Netherland was to wield absolute power, tempered by the privilege of appeal to the Amsterdam Chamber, thence to the Council of Nineteen, and thence to the States General, or government of the Netherlands itself. On important matters the Council of Nineteen had to consult the five separate chambers, and they in turn the directors and chief promoters in the large cities. Amid the confusion thus awakened by discussion, reference and counter reference, colonial affairs of a distinctly local sort were apt to meet with sorry consideration.

The charter bound the Company to "advance the peopling of those fruitful and unsettled parts, and to do all that the service of those countries and the profit and increase of trade shall require"; but the corporation chose to emphasize only the "profit and increase of trade." Colonization and agriculture were an afterthought. Being a quasi-public organization, it took up the struggle of the fatherland with Spain, and naturally regarded the plunder of Spanish treasure-ships as more desirable than

The Story of New Amsterdam

the comparatively trivial sum derived from the furs of New Netherland. Especially did the advantage accrue to the former when persistent neglect and other evidences of a bad economic policy made even the traffic in furs a financial loss. Had the settlers on Manhattan not evinced such sturdy courage and perseverance in coping with the obstacles offered by contact with the wilderness, with Indians and with jealous colonial neighbors, New Amsterdam must have perished soon after its foundation. Under a régime, now neglectful, now despotic, the history of what was at the outset a trading-post was bound to be rather uneventful, if not dull, until the time came when the conscious interests of an island community were to clash with the will of an imperious ruler.

The province of New Netherland having been dignified by the armorial insignia of a countship—a shield with a beaver surmounted by a count's coronet encircled with the words: "Sigillum Novi Belgii" ("Seal of New Belgium"), the Company proceeded to make good its claim to the country by actual occupation. In 1624 it sent out thirty families under Cap-

PLACCAET

By de Hooghmo: Heeren

Staten Generael der Vereenighde Nederlanden/
ghemaeckt op 'tbesluyt vande West-
Indische Compaignie.

IN 'sGRAVEN-HAGHE,
By Hillebrant Iacobsz, Ordinaris ende Ghesworen
Drucker vande Ho: Mo: Heeren Staten Generael.
Anno 1621.   Met Previlegie.

TITLE-PAGE OF THE EDICT OF THE STATES GENERAL OF THE
NETHERLANDS, CONCERNING THE ESTABLISHMENT
OF A WEST INDIA COMPANY, 1621
Courtesy of the New York Public Library

OCTROY,

By de Hooghe Mogende

Heeren Staten Generael/ verleent aende West-
Indische Compagnie / in date den derden
Junij 1621.

IN 'S GRAVEN-HAGHE,
By Hillebrant Iacobssz, Ordinaris ende Ghesworen
Drucker vande Ed: Mo: Heeren Staten van Hol-
landt eñ West-Vrieslandt. Anno 1621.

TITLE-PAGE OF THE CHARTER GRANTED TO THE
WEST INDIA COMPANY, JUNE 3, 1621
Courtesy of the New York Public Library

The Trading-Post

tain Cornelis Jacobsen May. The expedition arrived just in time to frustrate an attempt of the commander of a French vessel who was about to appropriate Manhattan in the name of the king of France. A Dutch sloop, rendered imposing by two cannon, promptly escorted the Frenchmen down the bay and saw them off at the Narrows. Then the little company sailed up the Hudson to the site of what is now Albany, where "they built and completed a fort called 'Orange.'"

In 1625 the Company dispatched vessels with horses, cattle, farming implements and seed, along with several families of emigrants. The animals were landed first at "Noten" (Nut, later Governor's) Island; but on account of the lack of pasture they were carried to Manhattan, where they throve on grass "as fine and long as one could wish." The goodly herbage for the beast had its counterpart in rich refreshment for man, since strawberries were so plentiful that people were accustomed "to lie down among them to eat them."

With the arrival of Peter Minuit as director general, May 4, 1626, the settlement of Man-

The Story *of* New Amsterdam

hattan began. A fort was "staked out," and families were brought southward from Fort Orange and northward from Fort Nassau, on the Delaware River, for whose temporary accommodation some thirty cabins "of the bark of trees" were built "on the east side of the river." The incipient stronghold was named "Fort Amsterdam" and the trading-post that it was designed to protect, "New Amsterdam."

Under Minuit systematic administration was introduced. It took the form of an adaptation of elements already existing in the fatherland to the actual needs of a small community planted for business purposes. The people whom Minuit ruled were regarded merely as servants of the Company. They could not hold land in their own right, trade with the Indians or engage in manufactures, except in their capacity as the Company's agents. A council was appointed to assist the director general in his task. Its members were Peter Byvelt, Jacob Elbertsen Wissinck, Jan Janssen Brouwer, Simon Dircksen Pos, and Reynert Harmennsen. Other officers chosen were the chief commissary, bookkeeper and secretary, known as the "koopman," Isaac

PORTION OF A LETTER WRITTEN AT AMSTERDAM, NOVEMBER 5,
1626, ANNOUNCING THE PURCHASE OF THE "ISLAND
MANHATTES FROM THE WILD MEN FOR
THE VALUE OF SIXTY GUILDERS"

*From a facsimile in the New York Public Library of
the original in the Rijks Archief at The Hague*

The Trading-Post

de Rasières by name, and a functionary called the "schout" who acted as sheriff, public prosecutor, inspector of customs, and on Sunday, as beadle and tithing-man. These duties were performed by one Jan Lampo. For spiritual needs the Company provided two "Krankbesoekers" or "Ziekentrosters"—a combination of lay reader and consoler of the sick—whose especial function it was to take the place of a clergyman by reading to the people on Sunday texts out of the Scripture, together with the creeds.

One of the early acts of the new governor was to strengthen by purchase the title of the Company already held by occupation. One may accredit him, therefore, with having made the first real-estate transaction on Manhattan to which civilized peoples were a party. On May 26, 1626, for the sum of sixty guilders, or about twenty-four dollars, paid in various kinds of alluring trinkets, he bought from the neighboring Indians the 22,000 acres on Manhattan at the rate approximately of ten acres for a cent.

Minuit's interest in real estate soon led him to put improvements on it. Under his super-

The Story *of* New Amsterdam

vision the fort, 300 feet long by 250 feet broad and flanked with four bastions, one of them faced with "good quarry" stone, was partially erected on the site of the United States' customhouse, just south of Bowling Green. According to the "koopman," the stronghold was to serve as a "battery that could command both rivers." Another structure to arise at this time was a mill for grinding grain by horse-power, since the settlers did not have the tools and apparatus necessary for putting up the usual Dutch windmill. The mill was located on South William Street near Pearl. Its loft fitted with rough benches served as a religious assembly-room. Here, in 1628, the Reverend Jonas Michaelius, the first clergyman in New Amsterdam, took charge of the services. He formed his first consistory with two elders, one of whom was Director General Minuit. The improvised church could then boast of fifty communicants.

Another building that bore witness to the governor's energy was a stone warehouse, thatched with reeds. Part of this edifice became the village store. Here Dutchmen and

The Trading-Post

Indians smoked their pipes and bargained for furs. Not far away the thirty dwellings straggled along the east side of Pearl Street. In the meadows facing the East River Minuit also laid out several farms or "bouweries" for the Company. These he stocked with cattle, sheep and hogs. The farms were tilled by the settlers, each of whom the Company furnished with the necessary animals. By 1628 the number of inhabitants had risen to 270.

Having due regard to the excellent commercial location of New Amsterdam, the director general began the industry of ship-building on a rather large scale. In 1631 he launched a vessel of 800 tons burden and equipped for carrying thirty guns. It was the largest ship built in America up to this time, and was even one of the largest in the world. Nearly two centuries elapsed before the shipwrights on Manhattan ventured to imitate the proportions of this pioneer craft of New Amsterdam.

Busied in the fur-trade, house-building and the common farming, the settlement throve. One unfortunate occurrence, however, that was destined to entail a terrible vengeance marred

The Story of New Amsterdam

this picture of quiet progress. The incident was the robbery and murder of an Indian by some of the Company's laborers near the large pond called variously the "Fresh Water" and the "Kalch Hoek" or "Shell Point," from a tiny cape projecting into it on which lay heaps of oyster shells. Later the name became anglicized into "The Collect." The pond covered the district now bounded by Baxter, White, Elm, Duane and Park Streets. Tradition had it that on darksome nights the lingerer by this pool heard the swishing paddles of a canoe propelled by a phantom chief. The tradition was prophetic, for in 1796 were heard in actuality the swishing paddles of John Fitch's tiny steamship, eighteen feet by six, propelling the forerunner of our ocean greyhounds about the pond at the lively rate of six miles an hour.

In 1633 Wouter van Twiller, formerly a clerk in the West India Company's warehouse in Amsterdam, entered upon the duties of director general. He is characterized by Brodhead, the historian of New York, as "deficient in the knowledge of men, inexperienced, incompetent and irresolute"; and Captain David

PORTION OF THE EARLIEST EXTANT ORIGINAL LETTER WRITTEN IN NEW AMSTERDAM.
JONAS MICHAELIUS TO JOANNES FOREEST, AUGUST 8, 1628

Dingham Versteeg, editor, Manhattan in 1628

The Trading-Post

Pietersen de Vries, his contemporary, declared that the Company had promoted van Twiller from a clerkship in old Amsterdam so that he might "act farces" in New Amsterdam. Yet within the limits of his ability the new governor certainly tried his best to serve his employers in their business venture.

Accompanying the director general were a number of soldiers to garrison the fort, and several notable civilians like Jacob van Couwenhoven and his brother-in-law, Govert Loockermans, a new domine in the person of the Reverend Everardus Bogardus, who came to succeed the Reverend Michaelius, and a schoolmaster named Adam Roelandsen. The educational efforts of the individual last mentioned appear to have been so ill requited financially that he had to take in washing at so much per year to eke out a livelihood!

The governor promptly formed his council, consisting of Jacob Janssen Hesse, Martin Gerritsen, Andreas Hudde, and Jacques Bentyn. The duties of "schout" were assumed by Conrad Notelman; but some difference appears in the assignment of the minor offices, that of secretary being separated from the functions of commissary and bookkeeper, the former going to Jan van Remund, and the latter to Cornelius van Tienhoven.

Realizing that the receipts from the fur business were not so large as might be desired, and had even shown a tendency of late to fall off, the Company ordered van Twiller to spare no expenditure at the central points of trade. The director general first turned his attention to the fort. During the interval since the departure of Minuit the earthen ramparts of that stronghold had suffered from the depredations of stray cattle that had wandered over them in quest of herbage. Having put the fort in partial repair, he proceeded to erect a guardhouse and barracks within the enclosure. Next he set up three windmills. One of them stood on Broadway between Liberty and Cortlandt Streets. The others he placed so near the buildings within the fort that the south wind was intercepted from their sails. Perhaps the slow and measured revolutions of the wingèd arms may have possessed peculiar charm for the placid van Twiller!

The Trading-Post

Pursuing his building operations further, the governor constructed for himself a brick mansion to comport with his official dignity, and various wooden dwelling-houses for the use of his subordinates, as well as for the smith, cooper and other artisans. Then on one of the Company's farms lying to the north of the fort he erected a bakery on Pearl Street near Whitehall, a brewery on Bridge Street between Broad and Whitehall, a boat-house and several barns. Another—the so-called "boschen bouwerie," or "farm in the woods," located at what was subsequently known as the village of Greenwich, and covering the site of a former Indian settlement—he converted into a tobacco plantation, the crop from which was the first successful yield from agriculture on Manhattan.

Like his predecessor, van Twiller evinced a commendable solicitude for the spiritual as well as the material interests of the community in his charge. The loft over the horse-mill he now replaced by a more commodious, if rather barn-like, structure to serve as a church. It was situated near Pearl Street, between Whitehall and Broad. The cemetery did not adjoin the church. That was laid out on West Broadway above Morris Street. For Domine Bogardus, also, he provided a house and stable on Whitehall Street near Bridge. The relations between the director and the domine, however, were not altogether friendly. Van Twiller's behavior on a certain occasion evoked a sounding rebuke from the clergyman, who called him a "child of the Devil" and menaced him with "such a shake from the pulpit as would make him shudder." The habits and temper of Bogardus himself, it might be said, were hardly such as to justify this display of ministerial wrath, which his enemies later declared to be "unbecoming a heathen, much less a Christian, letting alone a minister of the Gospel!"

For the commercial prosperity of Manhattan van Twiller had an especial eye. Here his views coincided with those of the Company, for the measure now to be adopted was probably aimed at the semi-independent "patroons" whose estates lay some distance up the North River. In 1633 he heightened the dignity as well as the importance of New Amsterdam by conferring upon it the so-called "staple right." By virtue of this

The Trading-Post

concession, vessels carrying merchandise up or down the river had to stop at New Amsterdam and pay duties whether they discharged their cargoes there or not.

About this time, furthermore, the first faint promise of Greater New York made its appearance in the connection of New Amsterdam with Brooklyn by means of a ferry between Peck Slip and the Wallabout. Near the former spot one Cornelius Dircksen tilled a farm. At the sound of a horn hung on a convenient tree the farmer hastened from his plow, and for a fare of three stivers in "wampum," about six cents (except in the case of Indians who had to pay double rates), rowed passengers to the Brooklyn shore.

So far as military arrangements were concerned, the governor did not always take due precaution. Captain de Vries returning from a voyage to Virginia arrived before dawn one morning and found the hamlet fast asleep. At daybreak he jokingly fired a salute of three guns, whereupon the slumbering garrison tumbled suddenly out of bed, "for in sooth they were not accustomed to have one come upon them so by surprise" and ran to their stations. The valiant

The Story of New Amsterdam

director general brought up the rear, flourishing a pistol in one hand while he vainly tried to dress himself with the other.

Apropos of this military episode another might be mentioned wherein a bad example occasionally set by van Twiller had a like effect on his subordinates. It seems that he held a farewell banquet in honor of Captain de Vries who was about to return to the fatherland. The festive event took place in a corner of the fort overlooking the bay, where the guests might enjoy the cooling breezes as they quaffed the bumpers of good fellowship. Rendered somewhat exuberant by the flow of spirits, alcoholic and intellectual, van Corlear, the trumpeter of the garrison, blew a loud blast that made everybody jump. Two of the Company's agents forthwith took umbrage at this unseemly conduct, and roundly upbraided the disturber. As skilled in fisticuffs as he was in music, van Corlear gave each of his critics a thrashing, whereat they ran home for their swords, breathing vengeance against the brawny trumpeter. Their rage, however, manifested itself, so the record states, "in many foolish words at the director's house," and

The Trading-Post

since their valor had time to evaporate during the night, when morning came, "they feared the trumpeter even more than they sought him."

Van Twiller, nevertheless, preserved good order in New Amsterdam. One Guysbert van Regenslander, for drawing a knife and threatening violence, was condemned to throw himself three times from the sailyard of a ship; and for slandering the governor Hendrik Jansen had to stand at the front door of the fort and ask pardon at the ringing of the bell.

Perhaps the most noteworthy feature of van Twiller's administration was his inauguration of private land grants. In several cases he made these cessions without the approval, and even without the knowledge, of the Cômpany. Hitherto that corporation had allowed only a tenancy-at-will. Under van Twiller, therefore, arose the system of private ownership of property on Manhattan. Of these grants two have especial interest. In 1636 Roelof Jansen, a former farm superintendent, obtained a tract of sixty-two acres, beginning about the present Warren Street and extending along Broadway as far as Duane Street, thence northwesterly to

The Story of New Amsterdam

Canal Street, the western boundary roughly coinciding with Greenwich Street. This was the origin of the famous "Trinity Church property."

The director general also made some grants to himself. One of them involved a purchase from the Indians of "Pagganck," or as the Dutch called it, "Noten Island." The name "Governor's Island," later assigned to it and erroneously ascribed to van Twiller's ownership, comes from the fact that, in 1698, the provincial legislature of New York reserved the island "for the benefit and accommodation of his majesty's governors and commanders-in-chief" as a military station. In 1800 the state of New York ceded it to the government of the United States.

CHAPTER II

THE VILLAGE

IN view of the rapid growth of the English colonies eastward and southward of New Netherland, an enlightened policy would demand that the settlement on Manhattan, as the heart of the province, be made more than a trading-station. So far the Dutch West India Company, anxious only for its profits in furs, had contributed little to the welfare of New Amsterdam. The settlement contained a roving, waterside population of sailors, longshoremen and traders, including many rough and shiftless characters whose main desire was to enrich themselves and go back to their native lands. A handful of soldiers tenanting a dilapidated fort and inclined besides to mutiny, the prevalence of dissension within and hostility without, the confusion and irregularity resulting from the double capacity of the director general, as an officer responsible to the Dutch gov-

The Story of New Amsterdam

ernment and as an agent of a trading corporation desirous of promoting its monopoly, were other obstacles to progress in the island community.

The mismanagement of the West India Company had become so apparent by 1638 that the Dutch authorities resolved to intervene for the establishment of such "effective order as should attract" the necessary colonists to New Netherland. Had the government gone further and assumed actual control of the province, the plight of New Amsterdam must have been radically changed for the better. The only step taken was to exert pressure on the Company to introduce the needful reforms. Too much had that corporation peopled the province with its own dependents, many of whom returning carried with them nothing "except a little in their purses, and a bad name for the country." The attitude of the States General forced the Company to understand how serious the situation was. Monopoly of trade had to be abolished and legitimate colonization encouraged.

Accordingly the announcement was made that henceforth freedom of trade would be per-

The Village

mitted with the Company's possessions in North America, provided that the traffic were carried on in the Company's vessels and rendered subject to the payment of freight charges, as well as of export and import duties. On its own part the Company agreed to convey all prospective colonists at its own cost and to give them a suitable amount of land, together with farm buildings, implements and cattle. The yearly rent demanded was a certain amount in money, or its equivalent, and eighty pounds of butter. The Company also declared its intention to provide and support ministers, schoolmasters, and consolers of the sick. On the other hand the emigrants must submit to the local regulations of the government in New Netherland, obey the commands of the Company, and allow all questions and differences that might arise to be decided "by the ordinary course of justice established in that country for the protection of the good and the punishment of the wicked." Under such conditions prosperity, based upon private enterprise and created by persons of substance, thrift and respectability, might be presumed to follow.

The Story *of* New Amsterdam

The successor to van Twiller in the post of director general was William Kieft. He was a man of considerable ability and experience, and possessed a good education which he displayed at times by allusions to classic authors. As an offset he appears to have been burdened with a large amount of self-conceit, inquisitiveness and rapacity, the opinion of New Englanders, that he was a "discreet and sober person," to the contrary notwithstanding. Though his activity and his temperate habits contrasted strongly with the traits of his predecessor, on the whole he showed himself to be quite as unfit to perform the duties of his office.

In the spring of 1638 the new governor landed at the floating dock, near the foot of the present Broad Street. Authorized by the Company to fix the number of his council, he did so in a way that gave credit to his ingenuity, while it heightened wondrously his self-importance. Though providing for three votes in the council, he permitted only two persons to constitute it: himself with two votes and Dr. John La Montagne, a French Huguenot physician, who had the privilege of always being in the minority, with one.

The Village

Among the other officials with whom Kieft surrounded himself were Cornelius van Tienhoven, as secretary, and Ulrich Lupold as "schout." A year later the functionary last named gave way to Cornelius van der Huyghens, a man, we are informed, "not to be trusted on account of his drinking, wherein all his science consists."

The condition of affairs in New Amsterdam might have daunted a ruler of less determination than Kieft. The fort almost in ruins, open at every side except at the one spot where it had been faced with stone, its guns lying prone upon the earth, other public structures in dilapidation, one of the three windmills running, the second out of repair, the third a wreck blackened by fire, the several farms of the Company neglected or thrown into pasturage, and their cattle everywhere dispersed—such was the forlorn state of affairs that confronted the astounded eye of the director general. And when he cast that eye upon the conduct of the people entrusted to his paternal care, amazement faded before the blast of reform that now swept over Manhattan. The local regulations and improvements of an autocrat were about to be inaugurated.

The Story *of* New Amsterdam

Salutary proclamations were issued forthwith. Written in a clear, bold hand, signed with appropriate flourishes, sealed imposingly and affixed in prominent places, these manifestoes in behalf of righteous conduct awoke the dwellers on Manhattan to a sense of duty, the like of which they had not known since the day of their arrival on its wooded shores. Having clearly in mind the multifarious population of New Amsterdam, now becoming a village, Kieft forbade rebellion, theft, perjury and calumny; exacted diligence and subordination; confined sailors to their vessels after nightfall, and compelled the inhabitants to show passports before they could leave the island. Displaying no partiality for soldiers over sailors, he levied fines upon the former for swearing, speaking scandal of a comrade, intoxication, absence from post, and firing a musket without orders. He also forbade the retailing of liquors, except by those who sold wine "at a decent price and in moderate quantities," and allowed the tapping of beer on Sunday only after church hours and before ten o'clock at night.

The Village

Another matter of vital importance to the community on Manhattan was the regulation of the currency. The specie of the time consisted of a few Dutch and foreign coins; but the common medium of exchange was beaver skins and "wampum" or "sewant." This primitive money, made from the inside of shells and strung together in the form of beads, early passed current at the rate of four beads for a stiver, or two cents. It was difficult to keep it up to the Manhattan standard of quality and value, since anyone who could find the shells could establish a mint of his own. Inferior "sewant" speedily appeared in circulation. So serious did the evil become that, between 1641 and 1662, no fewer than twelve ordinances were issued, fixing the value of "sewant," punishing its counterfeit, making it legal tender, declaring it merchandise, providing that it be paid out by measure, exempting it from import duties, and even authorizing its debasement at a certain ratio in stivers. Because there was so little actual coin, however, the circulation of the inferior grades of shell-money was not prohibited, lest "the laborers and boors (small farmers) and other common people having no other money would be great losers."

Outside of the realm of proclamation the director general gave careful heed to commerce and local industry. He caused a small redoubt to be erected on one of the headlands of Staten Island, and stationed there a few soldiers whose duty it was to notify the officials at New Amsterdam, by hoisting a flag, whenever vessels arrived in the lower bay—thus establishing the first marine signal-station within the limits of the harbor. In order, also, to remove the abuses in the cultivation of that staple commodity, Manhattan tobacco, which had injured the "high name it had gained in foreign countries," he appointed two inspectors of tobacco.

All suits at law and all public business transactions had to be drawn up by the provincial secretary, and duly attested by him. The reason for this arrangement the enemies of the governor later ascribed to his desire to prevent any testimony from ever being taken against him. The provincial secretary, himself an appointee of the director, assigned a different motive. "Most of

The Village

the people," he declared, "are country or seafaring men, who summon each other frequently before the court for small matters, while many of them can neither read nor write, nor testify intelligently, nor produce written evidence; and if some do produce it, it is sometimes written by a sailor or a boor, and is often wholly indistinct and repugnant to the meaning of those who had it written or made the statement. Consequently the director and council could not know the truth of matters as was proper, and as justice demanded."

To encourage the growth of stock-raising in conjunction with agriculture, Kieft provided for the establishment of two annual fairs, one for cattle and the other for hogs. These he ordered to be held at the "market house and plain before the fort," which plain became known later as the "Bowling Green."

Such efforts at promotion, and the comparatively large amount of freedom in thought and occupation enjoyed by the people of New Amsterdam, attracted many strangers. From New England came the folk who, disliking its ecclesiastical system, began to seek "the southern

The Story *of* New Amsterdam

parts," and from Virginia came redemptioners, i. e., indented laborers whose term of service had expired legally or voluntarily. These persons reinforced the governor in his policy of improving the conditions of agriculture. They bettered the method of raising tobacco, and set out orchards of cherry and peach trees. Upon the strangers, however, Kieft thought it prudent to impose an oath of allegiance and fidelity similar to that exacted from Dutch colonists. They must swear "to follow the Director or any one of the Council wherever they shall lead; faithfully to give instant warning of any treason or other detriment . . . that shall come to their knowledge; and to assist to the utmost of their power in defending and protecting with their blood and treasure the inhabitants . . . against all . . . enemies." In every respect the newcomers enjoyed the same privileges as Dutchmen. But as the number of such persons seemed to increase unduly, in 1642 the governor saw fit to forbid the inhabitants of Manhattan to harbor strangers, or to give them more than one meal or a single night's lodging, without notifying the authorities and furnishing the names of the visi-

The Village

tors. So large indeed became the population of English residents in New Amsterdam and elsewhere in the province, that an official interpreter was appointed in the person of George Baxter, an exile from New England.

The central position of Manhattan, furthermore, offered attractions to many transient visitors, who on account of the lack of accommodations elsewhere often had to be put up at the director general's house. So many of them came that their presence greatly inconvenienced that officer, who sometimes could afford them but "slender entertainment." Accordingly, in 1642, he decided to build at the Company's expense a "fine hotel of stone," called the "Harberg" or tavern. "It happened well for the travellers," dryly remarked Captain de Vries, who had dined with the director on several occasions, and doubtless knew whereof he spoke. The hotel stood on the bank of the East River in front of Coenties Slip, and was later converted into the "Stadthuys" or town hall. An imposing edifice it was for New Amsterdam, with its dimensions fifty feet square and its three stories in height, crowned by crow-step gables up which a truly venturesome chimney-sweep alone would dare to clamber.

In 1643 one Philip Gerritsen became the boniface of the tavern, and acquired the right to dispense the Company's choice brands of beer and liquors. As a means presumably of advertising his establishment, it appears that on a certain occasion mine host had invited a little party to sample his fare, when suddenly in strode a crowd of Englishmen, headed by a doughty Indian fighter, Captain John Underhill. In maudlin tones Underhill sought an invitation to join the festive party. On receiving a polite refusal, he insisted that one of the Dutchmen drink with him and his companions elsewhere. At a second refusal, the valiant captain and his crew pulled forth their swords and proceeded to carve up the metal objects on the tavern shelves, and to slash the doorposts, uttering boastful words withal to the terror of the ladies, when the "schout" with a small guard arrived, and ordered the roysterers out of the place. Underhill shouted: "If the Director came 'tis well; I would rather speak to a wise man than to a fool." Whereupon, remarks one of Gerritsen's guests, "in order

The Village

to prevent further mischief . . . we broke up our pleasant party before we intended."

In fulfilment of its promise to display greater care for the physical, mental and spiritual wants of the community on Manhattan, the Company dispatched two surgeons, Gerrit Schult and Hans Kiersted. These, together with Dr. La Montagne, furnished an array of medical talent sufficient to cope with all the ordinary ailments of New Amsterdam. As to educational needs, it will be recalled that the first official schoolmaster obtained renown from his deftness in whitening raiment rather than in that of brightening intellects. The new person selected for this versatile function had to be of "suitable qualifications to officiate as schoolmaster and chorister, possessing a knowledge of music, a good voice so as to be heard, an aptitude to teach others the science, and . . . be a good reader, writer, and arithmetician. . . . He should be of the reformed religion, a member of the church, bringing with him testimonials of his Christian character and conduct. . . . Whether married or unmarried he must not be under twenty-five nor over thirty-five." Specifying a few more of his needful accomplishments, he had to keep the books for the church council, read and pray with the sick, and assist the minister by turning the hour-glass in event of the sermon exceeding the proper length. A pedagogue so accomplished was found in the person of one Jan Stevenson, who began his labors in 1642. Non-official purveyors of knowledge, to be sure, did not have to possess such diverse qualifications. They needed only a fair amount of teaching ability, a license from the civil and ecclesiastical authorities, and in particular a talent for extracting tuition fees. One Adrian Jansen van Ilpendam started a private school in 1645, and for his instruction charged two beaver skins per annum. Generally speaking, however, these trainers of youthful ideas had to eke out their livelihood by financially more advantageous occupations.

Unfortunately this expansion of educational opportunities did not carry with it a corresponding expansion of space for school purposes beyond that available in private houses. The question of building a suitable schoolhouse was agitated in 1642, and, as the record expresses it, "the bowl went round a long time"; but the edifice was "built with words" only. The contributions for the purpose "found their way out," or more specifically, were spent by the governor during the Indian outbreaks.

Coincident with the project for erecting a schoolhouse was another for building a suitable church. The ecclesiastical barn near Pearl Street between Whitehall and Broad had become so dilapidated that Captain de Vries declared it was a shame that, when the English visited Manhattan, they "saw only a mean barn in which we preached." "The first thing they build in New England after their dwelling houses," urged de Vries, "is a fine church—we should do the like. . . . We have fine oak wood, good mountain stone, and excellent lime which we burn from oyster shells." This earnest appeal to civic pride elicited a ready response from the director general. But Kieft, who, according to de Vries, desired to leave a great name after him, put the query: "Who will oversee the work?"—this being a diplomatic method of asking: "Who will start a subscription?" De Vries, just as diplo-

The Story *of* New Amsterdam

matically, replied that he would give 100 guilders toward so worthy an object, provided that the governor himself would head the list. Nothing loth Kieft agreed to advance a thousand guilders on the Company's account.

At this juncture a timely event occurred, namely the wedding of Domine Bogardus' daughter. Here was an excellent opportunity offered to evoke generosity on the part of the large number of guests. After the "fourth or fifth round of drinking," we are told, the director set a liberal example of heading the subscription list as he had promised. The other guests, light in head and glad of heart, proceeded to render themselves light in pocket as well, by a proper mindfulness of the Scriptural injunction, "Go and do thou likewise"; hence they outvied one another in "subscribing richly." To be sure when some went home they "well repented it," but "nothing availed to excuse."

This episode has been described in a little rhyme entitled, "How the church of St. Nicholas was built: a legend of New Amsterdam." After telling of the preparations for the wedding, the verses run:

The Village

"It had long been the wish of the good Domine
To build a new church; for the old one, you see,
Was a barn, and at one time had been a horse-mill,
And to preach in it humbled the proud old man's will.
Now, the Domine thought, is the very best time
To start a subscription, and let each one sign.
The Director was there in his pomp and his pride,
With his worthy co-laborer, De Vries, by his side,
The Stevensens, Schuylers, Bayards, and Van Dycks,
Polhemuses, Cuylers, Van Winkles, Van Wycks,
De Kays and Van Cortlandts, the Banckers, Van Brughs,
De Meyers, Van Rensselaers, Kierstedes, De Trieux,
Van Horns, and Van Brummels, Van Dusens, Van Burens,
The Brinckerhoffs, Bleeckers, Van Dams, and Van Keurens,
The Dows and Van Breesteedes, Van Gaasbeecks, Van Duyns,

The Story of New Amsterdam

De Witts, and Van Geisons, Van Gansevoorts, Pruyns,
The Visschers, Van Vechtens, and more of renown,
The fairest and best of the little Dutch town.

. . . .

'Twas the Domine's chance the paper to seize
And lead off the list with Herr Kieft and De Vries;
And each in his turn would not be outdone
And promised to donate a generous sum.
So the money was raised in a very short time,
For the wily host managed that each one should sign.
When the guests realized on the following day
How much they had pledged, they were quite loth to pay;
But as honorable men they were bound by their word,
And it never would do to go back on the Lord."

The funds having thus been pledged, the director general appointed Captain de Vries, Jochem Pietersen Kuyter, and Jan Jansen Dam as superintendents of the construction of the church.

The Village

For security against the attacks of Indians, Kieft decided to locate the building within the enclosure of the fort. This arrangement was not at all popular. Since the church was to be built chiefly by public subscription, it ought to be placed where it would be most convenient of access. Aside from the significance of this argument, which showed that already population had begun to spread a bit beyond the extreme southern end of the island, other formidable objections were broached: first, that since the fort was already so small the inclusion of a church within its bounds would be verily a "fifth wheel to a wagon"; second, that such a comparatively lofty structure would take the wind off the grist-mill. To this argument of interception rejoinder was made that the breezes around Manhattan blew from more than one quarter of the compass. "Granted that the walls of the church shut off the wind from one direction," urged the advocates of location in the fort, "cannot the grist-mill grind with a southeast wind?" The sturdy defenders of the mill, however, would not be convinced, for they averred the mill had been too long neglected anyway. In consequence of its being idle, said they, it had become "considerably rotten, so that it can not be made to go with more than two arms!" Nonplussed by this argument, their opponents took refuge in pointed remarks about the readiness with which some people subscribed, and then forgot to pay!

The governor promptly terminated a difference of opinion which threatened to wax warm, and made a contract with two English stonemasons from Connecticut for the construction of a church edifice, 72 feet long, 50 feet broad, and 16 feet in the height of its walls, at a cost of 2,600 guilders. English carpenters also covered the roof with oak shingles which, by reason of exposure to the weather, soon "looked like slate." In the front wall the governor had a stone placed, with this commemorative inscription: "Anno Domini 1642, while William Kieft was Director General the community has had this temple built." When the fort was demolished, in 1790, the stone was removed to the belfry of the Reformed Dutch Church in Exchange Place, where unfortunately it was destroyed by fire in 1835.

Domine Bogardus forthwith took up his pas-

VRYHEDEN

By de Vergaderinghe van de Negenthiene vande Geoctroyeerde West-Indische Compagnie vergunt aen allen den ghenen / die eenighe Colonien in Nieu-Nederlandt sullen planten.

In het licht ghegheven

Om bekent te maken wat Profijten ende Voordeelen aldaer in Nieu-Nederlandt, voor de Coloniers ende der selver Patroonen ende Meesters, midtsgaders de Participanten, die de Colonien aldaer planten, zijn becomen.

Westindjen Kan syn Nederlands groot gewin.
Verkleynt s'vyands Macht brengt silver-platen in.

T'AMSTELREDAM,

By Marten Iansz Brandt Boeckvercooper / woonende by de nieuwe Kerck, in de Gereformeerde Catechismus. Anno 1630.

TITLE-PAGE OF THE "PRIVILEGES AND EXEMPTIONS" GRANTED BY THE WEST INDIA COMPANY, JUNE 7, 1629, FOR THE ENCCURAGEMENT OF COLONIZATION IN NEW NETHERLAND

Courtesy of the New York Public Library

The Village

toral work in a fortress of arms as well as in a fortress of faith. Indeed his preaching there seemed to be almost a matter of military conformity, as if he were the chaplain of an army at once carnal and spiritual. At this time, furthermore, his relations with the director general were rather more friendly than they had been with van Twiller. At the governor's special request he had remained in New Amsterdam, in order that "the increase of God's word might in no manner be prevented." The director general on his own part also inculcated a wholesome respect for the minister. One woman who had dared to ventilate her opinions about the domine somewhat too freely was compelled to appear in front of Fort Amsterdam at the sounding of the bell, and declare in the presence of the governor and council that she knew the minister to be an honest and pious man, and, with all the emphasis of seventeenth century tautology, to confess that she had "lied falsely."

Under the head of material improvements Kieft gave particular heed to placing the Company's "bouweries" in order, stocking them with cattle, and seeing that they were profitably leased. On account of its fine view of the East River he selected Pearl Street, then a road along the shore front, as the élite highway for the better class of dwellings. He also straightened the streets and improved their sanitary condition.

This reference to streets permits a brief digression upon the topography of New Amsterdam at the time. When the land on Manhattan had little value, private ownership of real property was virtually non-existent, and the population of the island was quite migratory in character, the first settlers had located themselves pretty much at will. Before the arrival of Kieft there had been no regulation of streets, and the thoroughfares had had no names, except those suggested by the nature of the ground and the like. Convenience in arriving at certain places, and in skirting hills or marshes, decided the course of the existing roads or lanes. Some even were mere cowpaths. The fact accounts for the narrow and crooked streets below Wall Street, and for some to the north of that financial highway. There were two principal roads, the first extending northward from the fort along what is now Broadway to the "Maagde

The Village

Paatje" or Maiden Lane—so named, perhaps, from the practice of the Dutch damsels of washing clothes in a rill that then ran through it. The second road began along the side of the fort at Whitehall Street, continued along Stone Street, crossed a small stream at Broad Street, where Bridge Street is now found, traversed the shore along Pearl Street to Hanover Square, and from that point made its way by Pearl Street along the river bank to Peck Slip, where the ferry to Brooklyn was located.

Although private ownership of land had begun in the time of van Twiller, it was not until 1642 that care in the location of boundaries and due regard for symmetry in alinement secured the appointment of Andreas Hudde as surveyor. Thereafter, when land was allotted or conveyed, rods and "morgens," or acres, defined its limits. In the same year occurred the first recorded sale of what might be termed a city lot, 110 feet in length by 30 feet in breadth, and situated on the present Bridge Street, for the price of 24 guilders. A grantee of a lot at the lower end of Broadway near Bowling Green was Martin Krigier, who built a tavern there. Near the corner of Pearl

The Story of New Amsterdam

and Wall Streets Guleyn Vigne tilled a farm. Another one belonging to Jan Jansen Dam, north of Wall Street, extended nearly across the island, while Secretary van Tienhoven's agricultural establishment stretched from Broadway to a spot between Maiden Lane and Ann Street. One Cornelius Clopper plied the trade of blacksmith on the corner of Pearl Street and Maiden Lane; hence the road passing in front of his forge, and traversing some marshy ground, received the name of "Smit's Vly" or "Swamp." Fulton Market of later times indeed was long known as the "Fly Market." Lying still further to the north came the plantation of the surveyor, Hudde, near Corlear's Hook, at the foot of Grand Street. Certain Virginians, also, George Holmes and Thomas Hall, laid out a tobacco plantation near "Deutel Bay," the word "deutel" meaning a peg by which casks were fastened, and alluding to the peg-like shape of the cove formed by the East River at the foot of East 45th Street. The English later converted the expression into "Turtle Bay." Dr. La Montagne's farm lay to the north of this locality, somewhere between Eighth Avenue and the Har-

The Village

lem River, and rejoiced in the appropriately rustic name of Vriedendael, or "Peaceful Valley." In all "ground-briefs," or patents for land, however, was inserted a clause that "stuck in the bosom" of everyone. This prescribed that the grantee should acknowledge the "noble lords of the Dutch West India Company as his masters, and should be obedient to the Director and Council and should submit . . . to all such taxes and imposts as may be . . . imposed by the noble lords."

Many evidences of wealth which would seem to justify taxation of at least the substantial inhabitants of New Amsterdam are furnished by the inventories contained in several wills probated at this time. One of them enumerates as family possessions: "forty books; eleven pictures; five guns; . . . silver cups, spoons, tankards, and bowls; thirty pewter plates; agricultural and brewing implements; divers specimens of bedding and clothing, such as satin, grogram, suits and gloves; a stone house covered with tiles; tobacco and outhouses; horses, cattle, and pigs." Another tells of "gold hoop rings, silver medals and chains; . . . silver brandy cups and goblets; Spanish leather patterns; a damask furred jacket; linen handkerchiefs, with lace, and brass warming pans." Quite edifying matter for reading, also, had the thousand or more dwellers on Manhattan: such as Luther's "Complete Catechism," the "Four Ends of Death" and "Fifty Pictures of Resurrection."

All these signs of prosperity and progress among the people of New Amsterdam had been preparing the way unconsciously for an assertion of their value to the community, which was to assume a form undreamed of by the Dutch West India Company or its zealous agent. Hitherto, because of their manifest utility, the proclamations of Director General Kieft had been obeyed without serious demur. Now, in an evil moment for autocrats and corporations, the governor aroused the latent sentiment of common interests to forcible expression.

The various measures taken by Kieft to define the relations between the white settlers and the Indians had been for the most part wise. For example, he had forbidden the sale of arms and ammunition to the natives. He had ordered all settlers whose lands adjoined those cultivated by

The Village

Indians to enclose their farms with suitable fences, hoping thus to obviate a frequent complaint of the natives that the white men's cattle injured their cornfields. He had warned his people also against excessive familiarity with their savage neighbors. Yet a foolish act of his own, no less than the imprudence of the settlers, brought on a catastrophe.

Under the plea of the great expense caused by the maintenance of soldiers and fortifications in New Netherland, Kieft proclaimed that the Indians, particularly those around Manhattan, "whom we have thu- far defended against their enemies," should pay a tribute of corn, furs and "sewant." In case of their refusal to do so, he threatened summary measures "to remove their reluctance."

Whether the director general's plea was sincere, whether, as was later charged against him, he was "trying to make a wrong record with the Company," or whether he simply regarded this step as an opportunity for personal enrichment, may never be known. It is highly probable that he expected an eventual, if grudging, obedience. Great must have been his amazement, therefore,

The Story *of* New Amsterdam

when he received a reply from the Indians, couched in their simple and straightforward language, wherein they "wondered how the sachem at the fort dared to exact such things from them. He must be a very shabby fellow; he had come to live in their land when they had not invited him, and now he came to deprive them of their corn for nothing. The soldiers at the fort did not protect the Indians when engaged in war with other tribes. At such a time the Indians crept together like cats upon a piece of cloth, and could be killed a thousand times before any tidings could arrive at the fort. They had allowed the Dutch to take possession of the country peaceably; they had never demanded anything for it, and therefore the Dutch were indebted to the Indians rather than the Indians to the Dutch. Moreover the Indians paid full price for everything they bought, and there was no reason why they should give the Hollanders corn for nothing. In conclusion," ran the reply, "if we have ceded to you the country you are living in, we yet remain masters of what we have kept for ourselves."

Less influenced by the rumor that the Indians

The Village

were trying to "poison the Director or to enchant him by their deviltry" than by the manifest temper of the savages, Kieft ordered the inhabitants of Manhattan to provide themselves with arms and to stand in readiness for any service. The precaution was justified, for this attempted levy of tribute, the hasty punishment of certain natives for a theft they had not committed, and the murder of a Dutch wheelwright by an Indian near Deutel Bay in revenge for the killing of his kinsman by some Dutchmen near the "Collect" several years before, were the direct causes of the coming war with the savages.

Perceiving that he would be held responsible for the consequences of any rash action, the governor determined to consult the opinion of the community, and request its advice and approval. This might enable him to offset occasional hints that had been made about his cowardice. "It was all very well for him," some bold spirits ventured to intimate, "him who could secure his own life in a good fort out of which he had not slept a single night." Accordingly, in August, 1641, he summoned all masters and heads of families in Manhattan and its vicinity to meet at Fort

The Story of New Amsterdam

Amsterdam "there to resolve on something of the first necessity." At this first mass-meeting on Manhattan the governor requested advice as to the best policy to be pursued, his motive clearly being to share, if not to shift, responsibility for any radical treatment of the Indians, or, as one contemporary record states, to have the people "serve as cloaks and catspaws." The assemblage proceeded to choose "twelve select men" to consider Kieft's proposals. This first body of popular representatives on Manhattan was composed of Jacques Bentyn, Maryn Adriaensen, Jan Jansen Dam, Hendrik Jansen, David Pietersen de Vries, Jacob Stoffelsen, Abram Molenaar, Frederick Lubbertsen, Jochem Pietersen Kuyter, Gerrit Dircksen, George Rapelje, and Abram Planck. They immediately elected Captain de Vries chairman. After suitable deliberation they agreed that the murder of the unoffending wheelwright ought to be avenged. Accordingly they asked the director general to make the necessary preparations, and, in particular, to procure a sufficient number of coats-of-mail "for the soldiers as well as for the freemen who are willing to pay their share of the

The Village

expenses." Since the governor, furthermore, was the military commander, he ought to lead the expedition.

Before any aggressive action was taken the Twelve Men, voicing the sentiments of a community that had remembered at last the free institutions of the fatherland, petitioned Kieft for a reorganization of the Council. The criticism and distrust awakened by the practice of the governor in choosing special advisers from subordinate agents of the Company, rather than from the worthy and competent people at large, explain the desire forthwith expressed for a council of at least five members, and the redress of a number of other grievances. Since the director general had obtained popular approval of his expedition against the Indians he could afford to make a few promises that he speedily forgot. He did not forget, however, to indulge in a proclamation thanking the Twelve Men for their advice, which would be adopted "with God's help and in fitting time"; and prohibited the further meeting of any popular assemblies without his express command, as tending to dangerous "consequences and to the great injury both

The Story *of* New Amsterdam

of the country and of our authority." The first manifestation of a village's civic spirit had ended in apparent failure.

Little having been accomplished in the expedition as planned, Kieft, encouraged by the warlike element in the community, ordered vengeance to be wreaked upon some parties of refugee Indians in the neighborhood, who had fled from their tribal enemies, the Mohawks. The barbarity that accompanied this massacre of helpless fugitives, men, women and children, evoked an outburst of ferocity on the part of the savages that repaid the debt of slaughter with horrible interest. The terror-stricken colonists crowded into the fort as the only place of refuge from their fierce enemies. For the director general it was not pleasant to suffer the wrath of the ruined, the widowed, the fatherless, and those bereft of their children. In one short week sorrow and desolation had swept over the island community, and now it was fitting time "to invoke from Heaven the mercy which the Christian had denied the heathen." The governor forthwith proclaimed a day of fasting and prayer. "We continue to suffer much trouble

The Village

and loss from the heathen, and many of our inhabitants see their lives and property in danger, which is doubtless owing to our sins," ran the proclamation. Everyone, accordingly, was exhorted penitently to supplicate the divine mercy, "so that the holy name may not through our iniquities be blasphemed by the heathen." The director general's inclination to charge the responsibility for the calamities upon his advisers, however, caused one of them, raging with anger, to confront him with drawn sword and loaded pistol. "What devilish lies are you reporting of me?" cried the would-be assassin, as he levelled the pistol. But Kieft's career did not stop then and there, for the bystanders interfered.

Again the governor was forced to consult the views of the community. In 1643 he called a popular meeting for the election of representatives to discuss the situation. The body of eight delegates chosen had quite a cosmopolitan character. Four nationalities were present in it: Dutch, in the persons of Jan Jansen Dam, Barent Dircksen, Abraham Pietersen and Gerrit Wolfertsen; German, Jochem Pietersen Kuyter; Belgian, Cornelius Melyn, and English, Thomas

Hall and Isaac Allerton. The board promptly excluded Jan Jansen Dam as one of the unlucky advisers of Kieft and chose one Jan Evertsen Bout to take his place. The Eight Men then resolved to equip a military force to cope with the river Indians, proposed the suppression of all "taverning" as well as other irregularities, and suggested a week of preaching instead; but a praiseworthy proclamation to this effect was not faithfully observed.

Once more the Indian conflict raged, and the terrified villagers flocked to the protecting ramparts of a fort become so dilapidated that to a disgusted critic it seemed "rather a mole-hill than a fortress against an enemy." Thereupon the Eight Men made a radical demand to the effect that the cargoes of two of the Company's ships, then loading for Curaçao, should be landed and a part of their crews drafted into military service; also that the director general should obtain help from the English in Connecticut, even if the province of New Netherland had to be given them as security. In reply to the first part of the demand the governor ordered the vessels to clear for Curaçao, bearing in their holds the very

The Village

commodities that the people of Manhattan themselves had raised, and for which the island community uttered almost a starving cry. The other portion of the demand was acceded to by sending two envoys to New Haven, but the English declined to do more than supply the Dutch with provisions. Exasperated by the conduct of Kieft, and rendered desperate by slaughter, destruction and famine, the Eight Men sent to the authorities in the Netherlands a memorial pathetically describing the plight of New Amsterdam and beseeching relief.

By this time the governor had aroused the hatred of the Indians no less than the detestation of the people of Manhattan. Indeed the savages are represented as crying daily for "Wouter, Wouter," meaning the placid and pacific Wouter van Twiller. But as soon as they had "stowed their maize into holes," says the record, they resumed their practice of murdering Dutchmen. The village, practically ruined, could not pay the soldiers at the fort, and the Dutch West India Company, rendered bankrupt by recent military fiascoes in Brazil, could do nothing. Kieft thereupon felt obliged to reconvene the Eight Men. To them he proposed the levy of an excise on wine, beer, brandy and beaver skins as a means of replenishing the treasury. The Eight Men promptly opposed the scheme as oppressive, illegal and arbitrary, for which presumption they were roundly censured. "I have more power here," declared the director general, "than the Company itself; therefore I may do and suffer in this country what I please. I am my own master, for I have my commission, not from the Company, but from the States General."

The inevitable proclamation followed. In it Kieft asserted that, acting on the advice of the Eight Men chosen by the community, he had decided to levy the excise in question "on those wares from which the good inhabitants will suffer the least inconvenience." When open discontent was shown, the governor sent for three of the Eight Men, but kept them waiting in his hall without an interview, so they returned "as wise as they came." Probably at the advice of the Eight Men the brewers refused to pay the tax, as not authorized by the people of New Amsterdam. This flame of liberty, kindled by the fric-

The Village

tion of an arbitrary will with the interests of the community, the director general strove to quench by copious draughts of the taxable beer, confiscated and given as a prize to the soldiers.

Whatever the outcome for the present, the villagers on Manhattan had learned a lesson in political rights, namely that of resistance to oppression. Those on the governor's side talked of "nothing else but of princely power and sovereignty . . . maintaining that the power of the Director was greater than that of his Highness of Orange [i. e. the Stadholder] in the Netherlands. . . . They could do nothing amiss, however bad it might be, while those opposed to him were always wrong in whatever they did well." On its part the community could afford to wait.

Meanwhile in his reports to the Company Kieft had tried to fasten the blame for all the misfortunes upon the people of New Amsterdam themselves, and particularly so in a "book ornamented with water-color drawings," which, in the opinion of the Eight Men, contained "as many lies as lines." "It would be well," observed the Eight Men in a memorial they now

The Story *of* New Amsterdam

sent, praying for the governor's recall, "to inquire how the Director General can so aptly write . . . since his honor . . . has constantly resided on the Manhattans, and has never been further from his kitchen and bedroom than the middle of the aforesaid island." The memorial proved effective. Kieft, after a salutary warning from the Company, became somewhat milder in his behavior and utterances. When in 1645 the Indians asked for peace he willingly granted it, and general rejoicing for the deed was manifested by a majestic salute of three guns from the fort. Summoning the people to assemble there at the ringing of the bell and the hoisting of the colors, in order to hear the articles of peace read, the governor went so far as to assure them that, "if anyone could give good advice, he might then declare his opinions freely."

But "the spit was soon turned in the ashes." Aware that the Company contemplated his recall, and aware also that the community knew it, Kieft was in no humor to tolerate personal remarks about him, especially from pugnacious persons who threatened to "fix" him as soon as he should "take off the coat with which he was bedecked by the lords his masters." Those who dared to speak freely he fined and banished without appeal to the fatherland, as causing "dangerous consequences to the supreme authority of this land's magistracy."

At length the domine espoused the popular cause. "What are the great men of the country," cried he, "but vessels of wrath and fountains of woe and trouble. They think of nothing but to plunder the property of others, to dismiss, to banish, and to transport to Holland." Kieft promptly retorted in kind. He denounced the minister as a tattler of "old wives' stories drawn out from a distaff, as a great cackler, and a seditious man withal who sought . . . to excite the people . . . against him who was their sovereign ruler." Unable, however, to escape the fulminations of clerical wrath, the governor absented himself altogether from church; and, in order to annoy the domine, encouraged the soldiers "to perform all kinds of noisy plays during the sermon, near and around the church, rolling nine-pins, dancing, singing, leaping, and other profane exercises." As this was ineffectual in lessening the domine's anger, he determined

The Story of New Amsterdam

to "out-thunder the man of God." He therefore ordered the drums to be beaten; but even as they rolled, the sonorous voice of the minister rose higher and higher and his words became still more defiant until, in sheer desperation, Kieft ordered the cannons fired, for the purpose, says one of his indignant opponents, "of going a-Maying so that a miserable villainy was perpetrated in order to disturb the congregation." But even the roar of guns could not silence the stentorian voice of the domine and its echo in the hearts of his congregation. Then, his patience all exhausted, Kieft haled the audacious Bogardus before the tribunal of governor and council. "Your conduct," snapped the director general, "stirs the people to mutiny and rebellion when they are already too much divided, causes schism and abuses in the church, and makes us a scorn, and a laughing-stock to our neighbors." Whatever the answer of the domine, the difference appears then to have been settled without further ado.

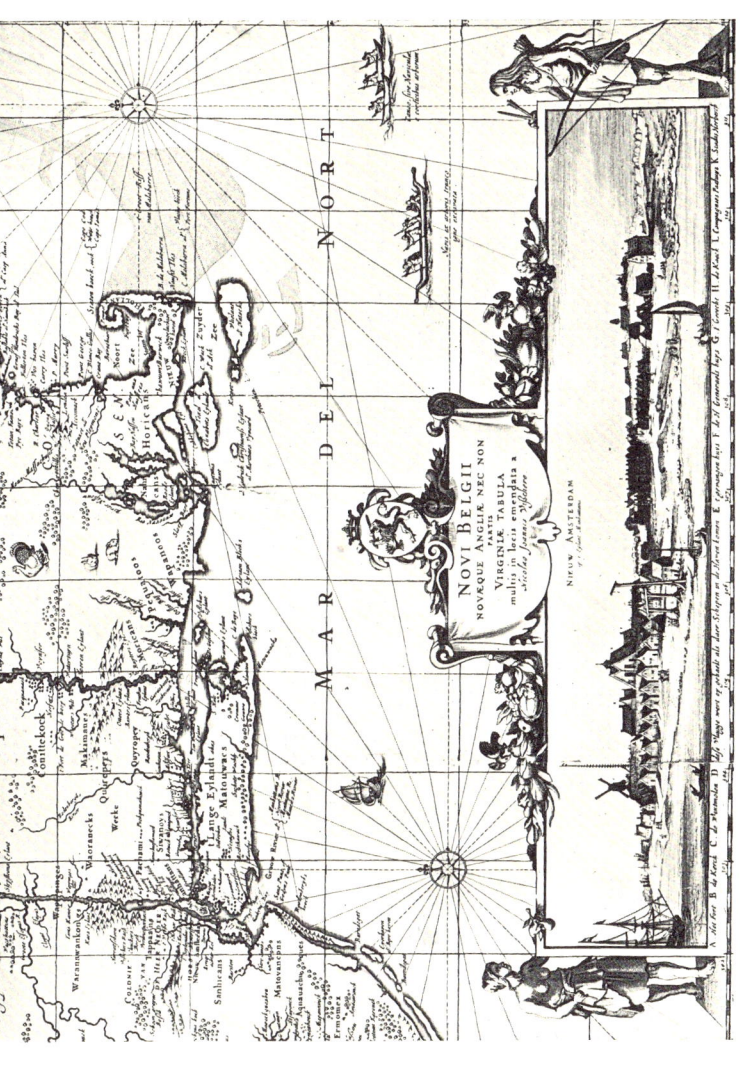

SECTION OF THE "VISSCHER MAP" OF NEW NETHERLAND, 1655, WITH A VIEW OF NEW AMSTERDAM
Adriaen vander Donck, Beschrijvinge van Nieuw Nederlandt. Amsterdam, 1656

CHAPTER III

THE TOWN

IN the year of grace, 1647, the good people of New Amsterdam doubtless dreamed as little of that village's future greatness as they were wont to suspect their English neighbors of honesty. Be this as it may, they certainly learned to distinguish their own welfare from the possible success of a trading-company. In the past their interests had been too much subordinated. "Things have gone on so badly and negligently." says a remonstrant "that nothing has ever been designed, understood, or done that gave appearance of content to the people; but on the contrary, what came from the community has . . . been mixed up with the affairs of the Company. . . . Very great discontent has sprung up on all sides against the expense and waste. . . . Moneys given by taxation have been privately appropriated. . . . Pride has ruled when justice dictated otherwise,

The Story of New Amsterdam

just as if it were disgraceful to follow advice, and as if everything should come from one head." The folk of Manhattan, therefore, were dissatisfied with the policy hitherto pursued by the Dutch West India Company and its provincial agents.

Stirred somewhat by the protests of the inhabitants themselves, and impelled to action by the warnings of the Dutch government, in 1645 the Company had determined to reorganize the provincial administration in New Netherland; and since New Amsterdam was still subject in all respects to the director general and his council, any change in the ruling body would be of much concern. It was eventually resolved that the power should be vested in a supreme council composed of a director general, a vice-director, and a "schout fiscal," or public prosecutor and sheriff. If by this arrangement the Company intended to modify the autocratic régime hitherto in force, and hence to employ the vice-director and "schout fiscal" as checks upon the director general, it did so only in appearance, for it knew the character of the person it now selected for the office of governor too well to sup-

The Town

pose that he would tolerate any encroachment upon his authority. That person was Peter Stuyvesant.

This vigorous and autocratic old soldier had filled for several years the post of governor in the Company's colony of Curaçao, and in an attack upon a Portuguese island had lost a leg. The missing member he had replaced by one of wood. His military career had imbued him with a martinet's desire for discipline and obedience to orders. A man of great decisiveness and strength of character, given over alike to prejudice and to passion, severe in morality and haughty in demeanor, with no inclination to conventional refinements, devoted to the service of the Company, his superiors, and yet thoroughly interested in the welfare of the community about to be entrusted to his care, Director General Stuyvesant was destined to show that he had a heart as big as an ox's and a head that would have set adamant to scorn.

In Stuyvesant's opinion the difference between bad government and good government did not lie in the contrast between paternal rule and popular control—the latter being the sheerest

The Story *of* New Amsterdam

nonsense; but between a selfish administration and an unselfish one. This leaning to paternalism in government was eventually to call forth the caustic comment: "the director hath so many particular qualities of which not one is serviceable in a desirable republic, that he is not fit to rule over Turkish slaves in the galleys, much less over free Christians." The civic spirit, indeed, that had begun to pervade the community under the rule of Kieft became especially active when stirred by the staff of an iron will or by the autocratic thumps of a wooden leg. And combat as he might, with imperious vigor and resolution, the popular efforts to restrain his paternal authority, he had to succumb, partially at least, to the determination of New Amsterdam that it would obtain the privileges known and enjoyed in the fatherland. Yet however ostentatious in command and arbitrary in conduct, Stuyvesant was never intentionally unjust or capricious, even if a rude warmth of affection and a real tenderness of sympathy concealed beneath a rough exterior did make him at times the instrument of unscrupulous advisers. If his rule far excelled that of his predecessors it was not because he was less of an autocrat, but because he had more honesty and more sense. Even when compelled by force of circumstances to relinquish some of his prerogatives, he remained throughout a man of masterful personality.

As the commissioned "redresser-general" of all grievances, Stuyvesant arrived at Manhattan in May, 1647—"like unto a peacock, with great state and pomp," observes a disgusted contemporary. In joyous anticipation of a liberal government the people of New Amsterdam fired such profuse salutes as to use up nearly all the powder in the fort. Some of the principal inhabitants then welcomed him with uncovered heads. Stuyvesant kept them standing several hours in this fashion while he had his hat on, "as if he were the Grand Duke of Muscovy, offering nobody a seat to sit down, although he himself had sat down at his ease in a chair in order the better to give audience." In this posture the new director general proceeded to enlighten the people of Manhattan on his principles of government. His utterances certainly were not those of a ruler who intended to be guided by public opinion; rather did they savor of benign paternalism. Desirous of being deferentially addressed as "Lord General"—a title "never before known here" says the same indignant commentator, Stuyvesant concluded his exposition of political science by the assurance: "I shall govern you as a father his children for the advantage of the chartered West India Company, and these burghers, and this land." Some inkling of forthcoming events might be gathered from the order in which these respective advantages appear. By way of benediction Stuyvesant "under the blue heaven" promised equal justice to all. Believing the occasion auspicious, Kieft, who had participated in the ceremonies of welcome, ventured to offer a few words of thanks to the community for their loyalty; but "some spoke out roundly that they did not thank him, nor had they reason to do so."

A short time after this popular installation Stuyvesant organized his council. Its members were van Dincklagen, the vice-director; van Dyck, the "schout fiscal"; Keyser, the commissary; Dr. La Montagne, the sole councillor of Kieft's régime; Captain Bryan Newton, an English military adventurer who had seen service in

The Town

Curaçao, and van Tienhoven, the provincial secretary. In addition to his advisory and other powers, the vice-director acted as chief justice of the province, with a reservation to the director general of final judgment in important cases. Such was the regular constituency of the supreme council; but occasionally other persons, like business agents of the Company, prominent sea captains when ashore, and in the event of great emergency, the chief citizens of New Amsterdam, might be summoned to attend its deliberations. The practice of appointing special councillors, it was said, insured to the governor a majority he might not otherwise obtain—"with their votes to accomplish his deviltry, and then advises with his ordinary council." The same authority declares that the majority of the council stood in absolute awe of the director general. Some, like Bryan Newton, were simple and inexperienced in law, and not understanding Dutch, "could and would say yes." Others were indebted to the governor or to the Company, and hence did not fare badly. Indeed one of them, though drawing a small salary as master of equipment, managed by strict economy to build a better dwelling-house than anybody else. How this happened, says the informant in question "is mysterious."

Of all the members of the council the one who roused the greatest amount of popular ire was the secretary, Cornelius van Tienhoven. He is described as "cautious, subtle, intelligent and sharp-witted," so expert in dissimulation "that he appears to be asleep, yet it is only in order to bite." More forcibly still he is likened to "an evil spirit scattering torpedoes." Said van Dyck, the "schout fiscal" to whose position van Tienhoven was later promoted: "Had an honorable person taken my place, I should not so much mind it; but here is a public, notorious and convicted fellow who has frequently come out of the tavern so full of strong drink that he was forced to lie down in the street, while the fault of drunkenness could not easily be imputed to me." Even worse offences were charged against this clever rascal, who appears to have exercised over Stuyvesant that occult and mysterious influence of the inferior over the superior mind. Not for a moment, however, is it to be supposed that the director general was a mere instrument in the hands of his secretary. To quote from contemporary testimony of what went on before the Director and his council: "If anything was said before the Director more than pleased him, very wicked and spiteful words were returned. Those who made it their business to speak to him . . . were, if he were in no good fit, very freely berated as clowns and bear-skinners." Indeed he "made it a personal matter against those who looked him in the eye." Such overbearing conduct frightened those who did not stand well with him from bringing matters before his court, since "whoever had him opposed had as much as the sun and moon against him." In this case he "bursts out . . . in such a fury and makes such gestures that it is frightful . . . yea, he rails out frequently at the councillors . . . with ill words which would better suit the fish-market than the council chamber. . . . But what shall we say else, of a man whose head is troubled and who has a screw loose?"

From the outset of his official career in New Amsterdam his adversaries acknowledged that Stuyvesant was ever "busy building, laying ma-

The Story of New Amsterdam

sonry, making, breaking, repairing and the like; but generally in matters of the Company." Nor does he appear to have been backward in his own behalf. "The Director is everything," complained his critics, "and does the business of the whole country, having several shops himself. . . . He is a brewer, is a part owner of ships, a merchant and a trader." But with all his multifarious interests Stuyvesant did not forget the welfare of the village on Manhattan. In order to promote it, he became addicted to the proclamation habit like his predecessor, although with rather more effective results.

The plight of New Amsterdam assuredly called for relief. Few were the "bouweries" under cultivation. Disorder and discontent roamed apace. Armed with a number of instructions from the Company, among which were commands to repair the fort, encourage the settlement and cultivation of Manhattan, and concentrate colonial trade at New Amsterdam by all available means, Stuyvesant entered briskly upon his task. One of the first of his ordinances dealt with the observance of the Sabbath. It runs: "Whereas we have observed and remarked the insolence of some of our inhabitants who are in the habit of getting drunk, fighting and smiting one another on the Lord's day of rest . . . in defiance of the magistrates, to the contempt and disregard of our person and authority, to the great annoyance of the neighborhood, and finally to the injuring and dishonoring of God's holy laws and commandments . . . we do charge, command and enjoin all tapsters, and inn-keepers, that on the Sabbath . . . before two o'clock in the afternoon, no liquors be sold except to persons travelling and to daily boarders that may from necessity be confined to their place of abode, under penalty of being deprived of their occupations, and fined six guilders for each person who shall have run up a score. Nor shall there be any selling after the ringing of the bell about nine o'clock." Also, for prudential reasons, "the selling, dealing out, or bartering in any way whatsoever, of strong drink to the Indians, or of permitting the same to be fetched by the mug directly or indirectly, even though it may be the third or fourth person," was absolutely prohibited under a severe penalty. Illicit trading, which injured the business of the Company as well as tended to interrupt the good understanding with the Indians, was likewise forbidden. Additional solicitude for the revenues of the Company revealed itself in port regulations designed to prevent smuggling. All vessels of a certain tonnage had to anchor henceforth under the guns of the fort near the "hand-board" at Coenties Slip; while those of a larger tonnage should locate themselves a few rods higher up the East River opposite the "Smits Vly," or South William Street. For violations of marine ordinances, indeed, the director general was much disposed to confiscate the offending craft—a fact that crippled commerce somewhat and provoked great dissatisfaction.

Nor had Stuyvesant an eye for the management of trade alone: his aesthetic sense was shocked by the untidiness and lack of symmetry that marked New Amsterdam. Pig-pens and chicken-coops in front of otherwise respectable residences, and the presence of domestic animals of the larger sort wandering nonchalantly about the crooked streets, were offences against the canons of a well-ordered village which must be removed. The governor, accordingly, appointed

The Town

three inspectors of buildings who were to correct straggling fences and zigzag streets by restricting houses and house-lots to their proper limits, and by securing improvement of lots within a given period. To check the migrations and depredations of cattle, the director general commanded the inhabitants properly to fence their farms, and authorized the construction of a pound for the harboring of stray animals. Finally, in order to replenish the treasury, and thereby to facilitate the construction of still more "laudable and necessary works," the governor saw fit to reimpose the excise on wines and liquors—much to the disgust of certain inhabitants who declared that "in a thousand ways it was sought to shear the sheep, though the wool was not yet grown." For the present at least Stuyvesant ignored the popular disapproval and turned to the performance of other serious duties.

It appears that Kuyter and Melyn, two of the Eight Men who had upheld the interests of New Amsterdam against the autocratic régime of Kieft, had the temerity to lay before Stuyvesant a formal arraignment of that administration, with a request for an investigation, on the basis of which they intended to take legal action in Holland. But if the rule of the previous director general should be subjected thus to popular condemnation, the same disposition might be made of his own. Should such a precedent be created, remarked Stuyvesant, "will not these cunning fellows, in order to usurp over us a more unlimited power, claim and assume in consequence even greater authority . . . should it turn out that our administration may not square in every respect with their whims?" "Forsooth," continued he, "these brutes may hereafter endeavor to knock me down also; but I will manage it so now that they will have their stomachs full for the future." He therefore affected to regard Kuyter and Melyn, though acting as prosecutors in behalf of the Eight Men, as merely private individuals engaged in a suit against Kieft. Otherwise it would be the crime of treason "to unite against the magistrates, whether there was cause or not." Kieft, accordingly, felt emboldened to come forward and deny absolutely the charges made by his accusers; and, says the aggrieved narrator, "his bare denial availed more than the community's men proved." The result was that the governor and council rendered judgment upon the unlucky Kuyter and Melyn instead. The decision stated that they had opposed and violated justice, threatened Director General Kieft with the gallows and the wheel; denied any subjection to the governor; called that officer a "duyvelkop" or "devil-head," and the greatest liar in the country; uttered mutinous and seditious words; and, to crown all, had shaken their fingers at the chief magistrate. A great legal writer, declared Stuyvesant, "hath held that he who threatens a magistrate or a clergyman even by a frown is guilty of assaulting him; how much more guilty then if he shakes his finger at him?" In the opinion of Stuyvesant and the council such offences were of great and serious importance, and not to be tolerated "in a well-ordered and governed republic, it being a matter of very evil consequence." The penalties of banishment and heavy fines were thereupon visited upon the popular tribunes. They also received a gratuitous warning against an appeal to the Dutch government. "If I knew, Melyn," said the director general grimly, "that you would divulge our sentence . . . I would cause you to be hanged immediately on the highest tree in New Netherland." That this prohibition of appeals from his decision to the home government was a part of his general policy, appears still more strongly on another occasion when he remarked: "It may during our administration be contemplated to appeal; but if anyone should do it, I will make him a foot shorter, and send the pieces to Holland, and let him appeal in that way."

This business disposed of, the needs of the treasury and the possibility of another Indian attack forced the governor, though sorely against his will, to allow a certain amount of popular representation in government. At the advice of the council he ordered an election to be held, in which the inhabitants of New Amsterdam and vicinity should choose eighteen "of the most notable, reasonable, honest and respectable persons among themselves." From this number the director general and the council would select nine, the particular function of whom, after their powers and duties had been carefully defined, was to advise and assist when called upon.

The Town

However limited their activities, the appearance of the Nine Men as an institution marked an appreciable advance toward local self-government and toward keeping arbitrary power within bounds. The assemblies of Twelve Men and of Eight Men had been called by Kieft to consider definite things, and had performed certain temporary services, whereas the board of Nine Men as now constituted might fairly be regarded as a more or less permanent body. To be sure it could meet only at the summons of the director general, and the hazardous experiment of electing the members by that "wavering multitude" known as the people was tried but once. Thereafter, at its annual meeting in December, the board should nominate a double number of persons from whom the governor would fill the vacancies caused by retiring members. Despite the restriction, this practically self-perpetuating body of nine represented with considerable ability the interests of the people, became an important element in the administration, and hastened the rise of the town of New Amsterdam. The names of the original Nine were: Augustine Heermans, Arnoldus van Hardenburg, Govert

Loockermans, Jan Jansen Dam, Jacob Wolfertsen van Couwenhoven, Hendrick Hendricksen Kip, Michael Jansen, Jan Evertsen Bout, and Thomas Hall.

The business laid before the first meeting of the board concerned repairs to the fort, the erection of a schoolhouse, toward the expense of which the Company would contribute in order to promote the "glorious work," the completion of the church, and the prevention of fire. Though several of these measures involved public taxation, the Nine Men approved all of them, except that relating to the fort. Since the community already had to pay customs duties, excises and tolls for grinding grain, the board maintained that the cost of repairing the fort ought to come out of the Company's revenues. The first session thus ended without serious dissension, even if the matter of the fort was "left sticking between them."

Nor was this the sole cause of discontent. Popular disapproval manifested itself against the collection of debts due to the Company so long as the claims of colonists for wages and grain continued unpaid. Public opinion criticised the

The Town

high customs duties and the readiness with which the director general seized suspected vessels. His traffic, moreover, with the Indians, which enabled him to sell them ammunition, while withholding the privilege from the people themselves, awakened so much indignation that, had Stuyvesant not produced his instructions from the Company authorizing the official sale in moderate quantities, and thereby calmed the fiery spirits in the community, "something extraordinary might have happened."

When the director general summoned the next meeting of the Nine Men, therefore, he found them ready with complaints and observations about the contrast between the "desolate and ruinous" state of New Amsterdam and the flourishing circumstances of its New England neighbors. The governor admitted the existence of the contrast, but asserted that he had only obeyed the Company's orders. The Nine Men proposed to dispatch a remonstrance to the Dutch government. Stuyvesant demanded the right to censor the message; but, as the board would not consent, "the matter . . . fell asleep" for a while. The Nine Men then asked for permission to confer with their constituents, a request which the director general promptly denied, but which denial they as promptly ignored. Such audacity made Stuyvesant wrathful beyond measure. Not satisfied with verbal denunciation of the Nine Men and their abettors as "clowns, rascals, liars, rebels, usurers, spendthrifts and the like," he brought suit against the ringleaders, seized the rough draft of a memorial to the Dutch government drawn up by Adrian van der Donck, who had now become one of the Nine Men, and threw that representative into prison.

Perhaps the governor's arbitrary conduct in this case had some personal justification. The memorial contained a few pointed remarks like: "Godly, honorable and intelligent rulers" should be provided "who are not very indigent, or indeed are not too covetous"; for a "covetous governor makes poor subjects," and a "good population will be the consequence of a good government." At all events van der Donck was soon summoned before a special council, but he could not "make it right in any way." Meanwhile the judgment against Kuyter and Melyn had been

SECTION OF MAP, 1630, SHOWING NEW NETHERLAND
AND ITS NEIGHBOR, NEW ENGLAND
*Joannes de Laet, Nieuwe Wereldt, ofte Beschrijvinghe
van West Indien, Leyden, 1630*

The Town

reversed by the Dutch government. They returned in triumph and, desiring that they should be "rung in" as they had been "rung out," asked that their official vindication be read by some of the Nine Men before the community assembled in the church. This privilege the director general felt obliged to grant, but he took care to notify the domine that otherwise no papers alluding to the government should be read from the pulpit unless they had been previously approved.

The memorial of the Nine Men was accordingly completed and sent to Holland in charge of three of their own number. Among other things the Nine Men petitioned the States General to assume direct control of New Netherland, and to provide for the erection of a popular government, such as that existing in the English colonies, "where neither patroons, nor lords, nor princes are known, but only the people." The memorial contained a statement relative to the need for a public school in New Amsterdam. This should have not fewer than two good masters, so that "first of all in so wild a community where there are many loose people, the youth be

The Story of New Amsterdam

well taught and brought up, not only in reading and writing, but likewise in the knowledge and fear of the Lord." An almshouse and an orphan asylum, also, were mentioned as desirable institutions for Manhattan.

With the desire of the Nine Men for an improvement in educational facilities the director general was in full accord. At the time they sent the memorial Stuyvesant requested the church authorities at Amsterdam to provide New Amsterdam with a "pious, well-qualified, and diligent" schoolmaster. One Willem Vestens appears to have met these requirements and, in conjunction with the local talent furnished by one Jan Cornelissen, began the task of stimulating the youthful intellect in Manhattan. The latter individual speedily developed traits of laziness and a particular fondness withal for the use of "hot and rebellious liquors," so his educational career came to a timely end. The Company further agreed to set aside a suitable amount of space in the village tavern for a school-room; but for some years the authorities at New Amsterdam seem to have found it impracticable to oust the loungers who had long puffed their

The Town

pipes, tippled their beer, and dozed in many a convenient nook. These self-appointed mentors of the community did not like to have their profound deliberations upon the religion and politics of New Amsterdam disturbed by the presence of round-eyed school children sitting solemnly on the narrow benches that ran along the wall, and perhaps, like their youthful posterity, stealing anon a furtive glance of admiration at the bold scapegrace, "zotscap" on head, who stood in the dunce's corner.

The care of souls was a matter of even greater interest than the provision of schools. This laudable work was intrusted to Domine Johannes Backerus, who succeeded Domine Bogardus in the pulpit of the church militant within the fort, at a salary of 1400 guilders. For some reason he appears to have become dissatisfied with his pastoral charge in New Amsterdam, and accordingly to have departed in 1649. One might seek the reason for his leaving in an utterance of the governor, elders and deacons, expressed shortly afterwards, to the effect that an "old, experienced, and godly minister" was desirable, "to the end that the very bewildered people might

The Story of New Amsterdam

not . . . be left in destitution." Fortunately Domine Megapolensis who had just come from up the river on his way back to Holland was induced by Stuyvesant to remain in New Amsterdam, partially on the plea that children were every Sunday presented for baptism, "sometimes one, sometimes two, yea sometimes three and four together," and partially for a consideration of 1200 guilders a year. In 1652, also, in response to the demands of cosmopolitan growth, came another minister, the Reverend Samuel Drisius, who was able to preach in three languages, Dutch, French and English.

On their own part the director general and the council ably seconded spiritual effort by Sabbath legislation, providing that "in the afternoon, as in the forenoon, there should be preaching of God's Word, and the usual exercises of Christian prayer and thanksgiving" . . . which all officers, "subjects and vassals were requested and charged to frequent and attend." At the same time they forbade all taverning, fishing, hunting, and other usual occupations to be carried on during divine service. Stuyvesant himself set a sonorous example of piety when he "sighed during the sermon so that he was heard by the whole church." The governor and council, furthermore, opposed any encroachment of civil upon ecclesiastical functions, for, when the proposition came up to appoint two orphanmasters, they declared that it was the business of the deacons to "keep their eyes open and look after widows and orphans."

Solicitude thus having been displayed for the minds and souls of the people of New Amsterdam, the director general and the council hearkened to the complaints of certain quasi-medical practitioners who manufactured and sold pills and "Vienna drink" (a compound of rhubarb, senna and port wine), and who resented the competition on shore of ship-barbers in the sometimes truly surgical art of shaving. To these complaints the authorities replied: "On the petition of the chirurgeons of New Amsterdam that none but they be allowed to shave," it is understood "that shaving doth not appertain exclusively to chirurgery, but is an appendix thereto; that no man can be prevented operating on himself nor to do another the friendly act, provided it is through courtesy, and not for gain, which is hereby forbidden. It is further ordered that ship-barbers shall not be allowed to dress any wounds or administer any potions on shore without the previous knowledge and special consent of the petitioners."

In this connection it might be mentioned that, in 1653, the governor and the council had to determine whether certain medicines were liquors and hence liable to an excise tax. One Peter de Feher, it seems, had petitioned them for permission to sell a decoction prepared by him for purely medicinal use. Since the applicant claimed many curative properties for his "wonderful water," the authorities granted the request, albeit with some misgivings. Aware of the propensity of their fellow men at times to value liquors for medicinal and other purposes, they expressed some doubt as to the legality of their consent, since "brewers and distillers were usually not permitted to sell at retail."

The subject, indeed, was only a minor phase of a very general question. Previous ordinances having been disregarded, Stuyvesant and the council proceded to issue a comprehensive one that thoroughly exposed the evils of the liquor

The Town

traffic. It lamented the fact that the "easy profits flowing" from this kind of business "divert and seduce many from their primitive calling . . . and they devote themselves to tapping . . . so much so that almost one full fourth part of . . . New Amsterdam hath become houses for the sale of brandy, tobacco and beer." No new tavern, therefore, was to be opened without the unanimous consent of the governor and the council. Existing innkeepers had to take up some other business at the expiration of four years, without the right of transference; they must report all cases of brawling to the authorities, and must maintain decent houses for the adornment of New Amsterdam. Nor did the possibility of pretending to supply a meal to those who wished to drink at unseasonable hours escape the vigilant observation of Stuyvesant and his councillors. "Whereas we notice and see," said they, "that former ordinances issued against the defraudations and smugglings practised with beer . . . are not observed, we hereby command and order that no inhabitant . . . shall be allowed to tap, sell, or give away beer, wine, or strong water by the small measure . . .

to table-boarders whom they may pretend to board, under which pretext we have seen many frauds perpetrated."

In addition to the drink problem regulation of the food supply demanded attention. A temporary scarcity of food and the nefarious practices of bakers led to the official injunction that bakers should make their bread of the "standard weight of the Fatherland," and should use "naught else than pure wheat and rye flour as it comes from the mill." The Indians around Manhattan, possessing fastidious palates, and preferring white bread to the ordinary black sort, paid for it in perfect sewant which the poor Europeans could not do. Because the "Indians and barbarous natives" were thus "better accommodated than the Christians," the director general and the council not only prescribed the manner of baking the staff of life, but fixed its price, and even forbade the sale of white bread or cakes. This they subsequently modified by limiting the prohibition to white cakes and cracknels. In order, also, to forestall any dearth of bread by reason of a poor harvest, they forbade under such cir-

The Town

cumstances the brewing of wheat and the exportation of bread and grain.

Trade and real estate also came up for consideration. In order to protect the business men of the island, "who by their freehold and birth are obliged to bear all the burdens," against the hurtful competition of merely transient traders, and to lessen the consequent drain on the supply of money, Stuyvesant and the council prescribed a permanent residence of three years and the possession of a "decent and habitable tenement" as prerequisites to the right of trade. Every Monday was set aside as a market-day, and an annual kirmess or fair to last ten days was established. Business, however, could not flourish as it should until the measures of size, weight and value had received the necessary regulation. "It is believed," remarks a contemporary, "that some" persons "of large consciences have two sets of weights and measures"; hence the authorities resolved to systemize matters by compelling the use of Amsterdam standards. Observing, moreover, that a large amount of the sewant in circulation was loose, unperforated, badly finished, and broken, or else made of stone, bone, glass, mussel-shells, horn and wood, the director general and the council demonetized such sewant, and declared the genuine article, when properly strung, to be a legal tender at an ascertained rate in stivers.

These local efforts to promote the economic welfare of New Amsterdam the Company supplemented by its orders to Stuyvesant to stimulate commerce, by which means "must the Manhattans prosper," its population increase, and its trade and navigation flourish. When the ships of New Amsterdam "ride on every part of the ocean, then numbers now looking thither with eager eyes will be allured to embark for it." Such was the prophecy addressed by merchants of old Amsterdam to merchants of New Amsterdam, a community of a thousand souls.

For the protection of real estate owners and their property, the director general and the council framed two appropriate ordinances. The first declared that, since contracts for land on Manhattan had become frequent of late, and in order to guard against fraud in the future, all sales of real estate must receive the approval of

The Town

the authorities. The second ordinance decreed that, since most of the houses in New Amsterdam were built of wood and thatched with reeds, some even having wooden chimneys, and that since the people had been careless in not keeping their chimneys clean, it had been decided to appoint four fire-wardens "to visit and inspect" the chimneys of all houses between the fort and the "Fresh Water," or the "Collect," i. e. between Bowling Green and Centre Street, approximately, at the present time. If the negligence of its owner caused a house to burn down, he was to be fined 25 guilders, and the proprietors of unclean chimneys were to be mulcted in the sum of three guilders, these amounts being devoted "to the maintenance of fire-ladders, hooks, and buckets." In 1651, indeed, Stuyvesant himself took such a personal interest in real estate that he purchased his famous "bouwerie" or farm, together with a dwelling house, barn, six cows, two horses and two young negroes. Bounded by what are today Third Avenue and the East River, Sixth and Sixteenth Streets, it furnished a name to one of New York's most cosmopolitan thoroughfares—the Bowery.

The Story of New Amsterdam

Turning from these acts of the provincial government to the events immediately preceding the rise of New Amsterdam as a town, it may be said that of all the articles contained in the remonstrance laid by the Nine Men before the authorities in Holland the most important was one that requested the establishment of a "suitable burgher government" on Manhattan, "such as their High Mightinesses should consider adapted . . . and resembling somewhat the laudable government of the Fatherland." The neighboring hamlets of Brooklyn and Gravesend had already obtained this privilege on a small scale; but since the Dutch West India Company had reserved the village on Manhattan as the seat of the director general of the entire province of New Netherland and his council, the local affairs of New Amsterdam had been managed by these officials alone. Although the representations of the Nine Men had induced the Dutch government, in 1650, practically to order the Company to grant New Amsterdam a separate administration, the command had not been obeyed. However disadvantageous on the whole both for the Company and for the island com-

The Town

munity the prevailing system might be after the growth of New Amsterdam had made it worthy of a separate government, the dread of possible friction between provincial and town authorities prevented for a while the municipal incorporation so much desired.

Meanwhile Stuyvesant had continued to wrangle with the Nine Men. So threatening did the attitude of some aggrieved spirits become that the council decreed that the director general should be regularly attended by a bodyguard of four halberdiers. Backed chiefly by the English element in the community, Stuyvesant deprived the Nine Men of their official pew in church, and expelled the vice-director from the council board for a satire against him, "stuck in the poor-box." "Our great Muscovy Duke," wrote the indignant vice-director to van der Donck in Holland, "keeps on as of old—something like the wolf, the longer he lives the worse he bites."

At length even Stuyvesant himself thought that the time had come for New Amsterdam to have separate powers of government, and informed the Company to that effect. Acting under pressure from the authorities in the

The Story *of* New Amsterdam

Netherlands, in April, 1652, that corporation replied as follows: "We have already connived as much as possible at the many impertinences of some restless spirits in the hope that they might be shamed by our discreetness and benevolence; but perceiving that all our kindnesses do not avail, we must therefore have recourse to God, Nature and Law. We accordingly . . . charge and command your Honors whenever you shall certainly discover any clandestine meetings, conventicles or machinations against our . . . government . . . that you proceed against such malignants in proportion to their crimes. We remark in many representations, though, of malversants that some hide themselves under this cloak; though we must believe and even see that they have not in reality so suffered; yet to stop the mouth of all the world we have resolved, on your Honor's proposition, to permit you hereby to erect . . . a bench of justice formed as much as possible after the custom of this city (Amsterdam). . . . And we presume that it will be sufficient at first to choose one schout, two burgomasters and five schepens (aldermen)." These officers were to form a municipal court

The Town

from the decision of which an appeal should lie to the provincial governor and council. In the choice of these magistrates, said the Company, "every attention must be paid to honest and respectable individuals who we hope can be found among the burghers."

New Amsterdam was now to gain recognition as a town, and in that capacity secure a government of its own, for which the island community had striven so long. But what was actually granted did not in fact resemble "as much as possible" that of old Amsterdam. At the outset Stuyvesant declared that the creation of the new town government diminished in no respect his own authority as director general. He construed the word "choose," as it appeared in his instructions from the Company, in such a manner as to reserve to himself the absolute appointment of the magistrates, contrary to the practice of popular election in the fatherland. He insisted upon the prerogative of himself and the council "to make ordinances and to publish particular interdicts" affecting New Amsterdam. He retained the right to collect and dispose of the municipal revenues. He even as-

The Story *of* New Amsterdam

serted his intention to preside at the meetings of the town fathers whenever in his opinion such a course was desirable, and in fact he often assisted at their deliberations, thumping imperiously on the floor with his wooden leg, when things did not go as he wished.

On February 2, 1653, Stuyvesant inaugurated town government in New Amsterdam by the appointment of Arendt van Hatten and Martin Krigier as burgomasters, Paulus Leendertsen van der Grist, Maximilian van Gheel, Allard Anthony, Willem Beeckman, and Peter Wolfertsen van Couwenhoven as schepens; while the director's prime favorite, Cornelius van Tienhoven was to add to his duties of provincial schout or sheriff those of the town as well, and Jacob Kip was made clerk. Of the burgomasters, van Hatten was a wealthy trader and Krigier captain of the burgher guard and proprietor of the tavern near Bowling Green. Of the schepens, van der Grist, a retired sea captain who had a fine house on Broadway below the present site of Trinity Church, plied the vocation of grocer and haberdasher, and van Couwenhoven was a tobacco planter. Beeckman, whose name is per-

FIRST PAGE OF THE OLDEST EXTANT RECORDS OF THE COURT OF BURGOMASTERS AND SCHEPENS OF NEW AMSTERDAM, FEBRUARY 6, 1653

Facsimile in the New York Public Library

petuated by William and Beekman Streets, was a tanner, and owned besides several farms, one of which lay in the neighborhood of a swamp now traversed by Beekman Street. Tenanted as of yore by tanners, the section is still called the "Swamp." Anthony was the agent of a large firm in Holland, and kept a store in the "ecclesiastical barn" erected by Director General van Twiller. Here he carried on a retail as well as a wholesale business, for it is said that on a certain occasion he sold a hanger to Jan van Cleef "for as much as Anthony's fowls could eat in six months." Jacob Kip tilled a farm of 150 acres fronting on the East River at Kip's Bay, at the foot of the present 34th Street.

The burgomasters and schepens announced that they would hold their regular sessions every Monday at nine in the building hitherto known as the village tavern, but henceforth to be named the "Stadthuys" or town hall, at Coenties Slip. After the meeting had been opened with prayer, the magistrates proceeded to civic business. Record-books were formally begun, and fines were imposed upon delinquent members: six stivers for tardiness of a half hour, twelve for tardiness of an hour, and forty for total absence. The burgomasters and schepens received no compensation other than the distinguished consideration of the community. A pew of honor having been set apart for them, every Sunday morning, preceded by that versatile functionary—the bell-ringer, court messenger, gravedigger, chorister, and janitor of the town hall, who bore in addition to his other burdens the magisterial cushions of state, the city fathers assembled at the town hall and, with Director General Stuyvesant at their head, marched in solemn procession to church. As a body the burgomasters and schepens issued ordinances and tried local suits and offences. The schout was presumed to execute their commands and also to serve as public prosecutor.

One of the early ordinances of the town fathers placed a suitable restraint upon importunate office-seekers the gratification of whom might influence politics. "Teunis Kraey orally requests, as he is an old burgher, that he may have the office of town crier. . . . It is answered: the petitioner may proceed . . . after the election, and then his prayer will be attended to."

The Town

Another ordinance was aimed against possible Gretna Greens for lovelorn swains and lasses. It recited that the proceedings of the court of Gravesend in "setting up and affixing banns of matrimony" between persons who had their domicile in and about New Amsterdam "greatly tend to infringement on the privilege and jurisdiction of this town, and prepare a way whereby . . . sons and daughters unwilling to obey their parents and guardians will, contrary to their wishes, secretly go and get married in such villages and elsewhere." The magistrates, therefore, took action to maintain the jurisdiction of New Amsterdam and to prevent unlawful marriages.

Among the early suits at law decided by the burgomasters and schepens was one in which Roelof Jansen sued Philip Geraerdy for damages in loss of time and in surgeon's fees arising from the alleged fact, as Jansen stated, that the defendant's dog had "bitten him in the day time." On his own behalf, the defendant declared that he had already tried to salve the wound by a gift of four pounds of butter, carried by his own wife, and was willing besides to give the plaintiff four guilders "as a charity." The judgment was so ordered.

As war was raging between England and the Netherlands at the time New Amsterdam secured a local government, the infant town was fortunate in having a man of military training as its guardian. The problem of defending Manhattan and the province at large against a possible attack by English neighbors, therefore, induced the governor to convene a joint session of the council, the burgomasters and schepens at the city hall. After due deliberation the assemblage resolved that the citizens should mount guard nightly; that Fort Amsterdam should be repaired; and that, since the stronghold in question was not large enough to shelter all the inhabitants, the town should be enclosed between the East River and the Hudson by a ditch, a palisade and a rampart.

Organized early in Stuyvesant's administration, the burgher guard consisted of two companies, one under the blue flag, the other under the orange. Its officers were appointed by the director general and the council from a double number chosen by the rank and file. As to the

The Town

matter of repairing the fort, the Company had already instructed Stuyvesant to bolster it up with "good clay, earth and firm sods." That corporation of course did not know that the herbage growing on the earthen mounds of the fort was very attractive to cattle, horses, pigs and goats that browsed along the ridges and gazed as they munched at the martial spectacle beneath them. The damage to the stability of the structure, indeed, caused by the depredations of rooters and ruminants led the director general repeatedly to warn the inhabitants of New Amsterdam against allowing their animals to run at large. "We see with great grief," observed Stuyvesant, "the injury done to the walls of the fort by pigs, especially . . . in the spring when the grass comes out. . . . To our trouble and shame we see the pigs daily on the walls busy with their destruction. Therefore we request burgomasters and schepens to . . . fence in the fort . . . and prevent the pigs."

In order to meet the expense entailed by the project of fortifying New Amsterdam, the local government resolved to raise 6000 guilders by a loan from the leading citizens, who were to be repaid by a tax upon the community. A contract was thereupon made with one Thomas Baxter to undertake the building of the proposed palisades and their adjuncts. The idea was to construct a wall across the island at the northern limit of the town, as a defence against hostile forces that might land above. This should consist of a line of round palisades, twelve feet in height and several inches in diameter, strengthened at intervals of a rod by stout posts to which split rails were fastened. Back of the wall a ditch was to be dug, and the dirt from it thrown up against the palisades. This sloping earthwork four feet high would serve as a platform on which the defenders might stand and overlook the stockade. The wall in fact ran along the East River to the so-called "Water-gate" near the junction of the present Pearl and Wall Streets; it followed the line of Wall Street—its future namesake—to the "Land-gate" at the corner of Broadway; and thence it proceeded westward to a steep bluff overlooking the Hudson near Greenwich Street. The strength of the wall, however, was never destined to be put to the test of war.

CHAPTER IV

THE MUNICIPALITY

THE establishment of the town of New Amsterdam certainly attested the public spirit and the zealous perseverance of its inhabitants, even if they had secured only a semblance of local self-government, a municipal framework similar in aspect to that of a Dutch town, but devoid of its popular characteristics. So long as the director general and council, acting in the name of the Dutch West India Company, remained supreme in the management of town affairs, the mere creation of a body of burgomasters and schepens meant little more than an increase in the number of officials, and a possible enlargement of the public burdens for their maintenance. The people of the youthful town, on the other hand, wished to enjoy a proper share in government. To do so they had to assert municipal individualism against the will of an autocratic governor and his council, and they had to extort from a grudging commercial corporation an acknowledgment of certain civic rights which would leave to the director general and his employers in Holland only a proper degree of supervision and regulation.

As an illustration of the difficulties that lay in the way of public-spirited deeds and utterances, two communications, one from the Company, the other from Stuyvesant and the council, to the town magistrates might be quoted. Said the Company: "It is the height of presumption in the people to protest against the government; so rulers debauch their authority when they pay wordy attention to it, and do not punish them as they deserve. . . . Conduct yourselves quietly and peaceably, submit yourselves to the government placed over you, and in no wise allow yourselves to hold particular convention . . . in deliberation on affairs of state which do not appertain to you." On their part the director general and the council reminded the town magistrates of their very subordinate position in the management of New Amsterdam affairs. Said they: "The establishing of an inferior court of

The Municipality

justice under the name . . . of schout, burgomasters, and schepens does in no wise infringe on or diminish the power and authority of the director general and council to enact any ordinances . . . which tend to the best interest of the inhabitants. What is solely the qualifications of the schout, burgomasters and schepens, and for what purpose they are appointed, appear sufficiently from the instruction given to them, by which they have to abide and conform themselves."

Despite the wrathful demeanor of Stuyvesant, the irate thumps of his wooden leg and the distant scoldings of the Company, the town of New Amsterdam contended bravely for rights of government along two lines that best displayed its individuality, namely, the election of officers and the control of the purse. When these had been attained and rendered conformable to the practice of the cities of the fatherland, the municipal structure of New Amsterdam would be fairly complete. For the time being, however, the people could not choose their own officers; the town itself had no revenues; the magistrates, appointed by the director general and the coun-

The Story of New Amsterdam

cil, had no authority to impose any kind of a tax without the consent of the provincial government; and town ordinances, as well as other manifestations of municipal activity, were liable to modification and overruling.

Shortly after the formal organization of the town had been effected, the director general requested an increase in its contribution for the repair of the fort. The burgomasters and schepens ventured to return a negative answer, with the observation that they were "altogether in the background." Stuyvesant then resolved to test the sentiment of the community on the question. He found it solidly arrayed on the side of the town magistrates. The expenses for the maintenance of military works should be defrayed out of the regular provincial revenue, said the burghers. At all events they would grant nothing until the director general should give the town a revenue of its own by making over to it the excise on liquors. This proposition Stuyvesant flatly declined to entertain, surmising perhaps that such an encroachment on the provincial treasury would be an entering wedge for other kinds of municipal claims.

The Municipality

Later, taking into consideration the possibility that the war between England and the Netherlands might reach their respective colonies at any moment, the governor saw fit to modify his attitude. Before a public assembly he offered to surrender part of the excise if the town would support the clergymen, the schoolmaster and the secretary. Believing the moment opportune, certain enterprising spirits now petitioned the director general to appoint a separate schout for New Amsterdam. Their belief was not well founded. Stuyvesant would consider but one radical scheme at a time. He agreed to relinquish to the town that portion of the excise which was levied upon liquors actually consumed in New Amsterdam, though solely on condition that the local government should contribute substantially to the repair of the fort, take care of the civil and ecclesiastical officers, and let out the collection of the excise to the highest bidder.

The success attained in this skirmish with the director general emboldened the citizens of Manhattan and vicinity to call a popular convention. It met at the town hall, in November, 1653, ostensibly to discuss measures for protecting the

The Story of New Amsterdam

inhabitants against pirates and Indians. After some conference the members invited Stuyvesant to a banquet at which they informed the astounded director general that they would meet again next month, and that he might "then do as he pleased, and prevent it if he could." Encouraged by this expression of public opinion, the magistrates of New Amsterdam on their own part administered a further shock to the governor. They notified him of their intention to send a memorial to the Company, and requested him to summon a convention still more representative of Manhattan and its neighborhood. Since this gathering would rest on an official basis, it could promote more effectually the preparation of the address in question. Realizing that for the moment he was helpless, Stuyvesant grudgingly consented; but his suspicion of popular movements led him to remark that these proceedings "smelt of rebellion and of contempt of his high authority and commission."

The "Landdag" or convention thus brought together met in December, and laid before Stuyvesant the heads of its memorial, which dilated upon the alleged maladministration of the prov-

The Municipality

ince and called for the redress of certain specified grievances. This effrontery was too much for the doughty old governor. He characterized the convention as a few "unqualified delegates who assume without authority the name and title of commonalty." Under that designation they had no right to address the director general or anyone else. Taking up one of the matters of grievance, Stuyvesant asserted that, if the "nomination and election of magistrates should be left to the populace who were the most interested, then each would vote for one of his own stamp; the thief for a thief, the rogue, the tippler and the smuggler for his brother in iniquity, so that he may enjoy more latitude in vice and fraud." But as the convention, heedless of the censure, affirmed its purpose to appeal from his opinion, Stuyvesant unceremoniously bade the delegates disperse "on pain of our highest displeasure." "We derive our authority from God and the Company, not from a few ignorant subjects," was the parting blast from the director general.

On December 24, 1653, the burgomasters and schepens dispatched their memorial to the Company, praying for a more liberal allowance of

The Story *of* New Amsterdam

municipal privileges. They requested that the office of town schout be made separate from that of the province, and that they be granted the power to collect for municipal purposes all of the excise levied upon liquors in New Amsterdam. Since even that would be insufficient to pay salaries and meet the various needs of the town, the authority to impose other taxes was desired. The magistrates petitioned, also, for the right to let out on contract the ferry between New Amsterdam and Brooklyn, to convey land, to have a seal distinct from that of the province of New Netherland, and lastly to have a special "stadthuys" or town hall, unless the Company felt disposed to donate the existing structure.

Having started their manifesto on its way to the Company, the burgomasters and schepens asked Stuyvesant for permission to imitate the electoral custom of the fatherland so far as to lay before him a double list of names from which he might be pleased to select the magistrates for the ensuing year. Incidentally they requested that the town fathers be given an emolument for their services more substantial than that of pretentious titles and distinguished consideration.

The Municipality

As to the first item, the director general merely reappointed the outgoing officials, with one or two changes; as to the second, he fixed the salary of the burgomasters at 350 guilders, and that of the schepens at 250 guilders a year, to be paid out of the municipal treasury. In this concession there was a touch of irony. Owing to the scant state of the treasury during the early stages of the town's growth, the payment of salaries was decidedly irregular, otherwise the town fathers would not have applied, as they did on a certain occasion, "for the arrears of their salary so long forgotten, in order that once seeing the fruits of their labors, they might be encouraged to still greater zeal." For a while at least they had to eke out their municipal stipends in dignity, titles and grumbling.

When an irascible notary ruffled by an adverse decision inveighed against the magistrates as "simpletons and blockheads," he was compelled to beg pardon, "with uncovered head, of God, Justice, and the Worshipful Court," as well as to pay a round sum in fines. Undaunted by this punishment, the same individual called the secretary a "rascal," who, much aggrieved by this epithet, "which affected his honor being tender," demanded "honorable and profitable reparation." Again was the notary fined for his intemperate language as a warning to slanderers "who for trifles have constantly in their mouths curses and abuses of other honorable people." Upon what seemed righteous provocation, strong language might be used even by the town fathers themselves. A poor widow happened to have her house sold under judicial proceedings. In desperation at the loss of her home she indignantly characterized the sheriff's deputies thus: "Ye despoilers, ye blood-suckers! Ye have not sold but given away my house." On the complaint of the officers that the exasperated woman's words were a "sting that could not be endured," the burgomasters and schepens solemnly condemned her utterances as "foul, villainous, injurious, infamous, blasphemous, insulting, and affronting," and as such meriting a severe reprimand, which was duly inflicted.

While on the subject of judicial proceedings it might be said that a particularly litigious notary and legal practitioner of New Amsterdam, named Solomon La Chair, had a mania for per-

The Municipality

sonally conducted lawsuits which placed him quite frequently in the posture of defendant. At one time suit was brought against him for the balance due on a house and for a can of sugared wine. On the stand he testified that he had intended to pay, but that somehow the money had "dropped through his fingers." This plea the municipal court admitted to be ingenuous, though not especially convincing, and ordered him to pay up at once. He appears not to have relished the decision, and while in this mood made the fire inspectors partial recipients of his contempt for the entire official fraternity by dubbing them "chimney sweeps." Fined for this remark, he wreaked wordy vengeance on the bailiff who came to collect the fine by calling him a "little cock, booted and spurred."

Perhaps the choleric temperament of New Amsterdam notaries was due quite as much to their slender fees as to their litigious inclinations. The legal Solomon above mentioned, if not equalling his earlier namesake in the ability to decide partition cases, did not, on the other hand, enjoy so large a remuneration. For professional services on one occasion he received as much as

The Story of New Amsterdam

ten dollars in "gray peas," and at another time was rewarded with an "English book of no use." Though history tells of how much this seventeenth century Solomon received, even to the extent of "gray peas," it fails to furnish enlightenment on a more interesting question, namely, how much he charged! What might be called the "vegetable item" indeed, appears in more than one judicial action in New Amsterdam. A certain Mesaack Martens, for example, having stolen some cabbages from the garden of Pieter Jansen was condemned to stand in the pillory with his head encircled by cabbages—a punishment doubtless intended to fit the offence, and not to indicate a possible resemblance between the head and its decorations!

After this digression upon matters judicial it would be well to note the opinion of the Company on the pleas of New Amsterdam for redress of grievances. Regarding them it wrote to Stuyvesant: "We are unable to discover . . . one single point to justify complaint. . . . You ought to have acted with more vigor against the ringleaders of the gang, and not have condescended to answer protests with protests, and

The Municipality

then have passed all by without further notice. . . . It is therefore our express command that you punish what has occurred as it deserves, so that others may be deterred in future from following such examples." The Company, nevertheless, proceeded to grant several of the requests. It authorized the separation of the office of municipal schout from that of the provincial schout, but denied to the town magistrates the privilege of participating in the choice of the new officer. It granted, also, the whole of the excise to the town on condition that it fulfill its previous obligations; permitted the municipality to impose other taxes with the consent of the provincial government and of the commonalty; vested the town with powers over real estate, and formally authorized the use of the "stadthuys" for local purposes.

So liberal a recognition of municipal claims the magistrates of New Amsterdam hastened to acknowledge, and at the same time repudiated earnestly any thought of disloyalty. Said the burgomasters and schepens: "We have never thought of anything but of discharging our duties to the utmost," and of displaying "to the best of our ability the situation and necessity of this country." Stuyvesant, however, placed little confidence in this protestation of civic virtue. He did in fact appoint a special town schout; but when the appointee declined to serve, he allowed the provincial officer, Cornelius van Tienhoven, to hold over in spite of remonstrances against this violation of the Company's orders.

Before long the director general complained that the burgomasters and schepens had been "prodigal of fine promises without any succeeding action." In response to his demand for an account of the receipts and disbursements from the excise, the magistrates estimated the town's expenditure at 16,000 guilders "for outside and inside works," and agreed to contribute 3000 guilders toward objects mentioned by the governor, provided that the town be empowered to levy a tax on real estate. Stuyvesant roundly berated the local officers for laxness of duty, declaring that the provincial government would resume its control of the excise and let it out for the benefit of the Company. He also announced that the provincial authorities would themselves insure the fulfilment of the obligations origi-

The Municipality

nally undertaken by the town when it was given the excise, and to that end would impose taxes on real estate, neat cattle, and exports in New Amsterdam as well as in the province at large.

Thoroughly aroused over the prospective loss of the excise, the first and only independent revenue that the town had ever enjoyed, the burgomasters and schepens forthwith offered to support at municipal expense one of the ministers, a schoolmaster and precentor, a "dog-whipper," or beadle and sexton, the schout, the secretary, the court messenger, and finally themselves into the bargain, if only they were allowed to retain control of the excise and levy the proposed assessment on real estate. For the maintenance of the soldiers at the fort, they affirmed that they could not provide, since they had already "continually engaged in the general works, submitting to watchings, and other heavy burdens," and had often demonstrated their bravery and willingness in times of calamity. Stuyvesant expressed some incredulity as to the truth of this assertion, and remarked that the quota of 3000 guilders was not large enough. He then proceeded to carry his declarations into effect.

The Story of New Amsterdam

Once more the town magistrates carried their plaints to the Company, only to find it less liberally disposed than before. As on the previous occasion, the Company chided Stuyvesant for not having used his authority as he should have done, and bade him enforce the collection of taxes even against the will of the community, so that "these men shall no longer indulge themselves in the visionary dream that contributions cannot be levied without their assent." To the town officials themselves it addressed the following reproof: "Honorable, Worshipful, Upright, Beloved, Faithful: As good governments are bound to take care that their lands, cities and peoples be free and protected as much as possible from violence and injury on the part of . . . enemies and neighbors, so it is the duty of a good commonalty to assist in defraying the common burthens which were contracted . . . for maintaining themselves therein. . . . Your Worships have . . . failed to procure any subsidies for this purpose. Inasmuch as that is contrary to the maxims of all well regulated . . . cities . . . it becomes necessary . . . that . . . no further postponement be made. . . . We enjoin this

THE SEAL OF NEW AMSTERDAM
Courtesy of the New York Historical Society

The Municipality

especially upon your Worships, with serious and earnest recommendation, not only to set a good example to the commonalty in contributing the aforesaid supplies, but also to encourage them therein . . . for such we find to be for the best advantage of the state." Here the matter rested, while the director general made preparations for a trip to the West Indies in the commercial interests of the province.

Just before Stuyvesant sailed, in December, 1654, the burgomasters and schepens resolved to tender him the official courtesy of a "gay repast" at the city hall. On this festive occasion the governor, on behalf of the Dutch West India Company presented to Martin Krigier, the presiding burgomaster, the formal seal of New Amsterdam so long desired. Heraldically described, it had an "argent per pale, with three crosses saltire; for a crest a beaver proper surmounted by a mantle on which was a shield argent bearing the letters G. W. C. (Geoctroiuyeerde West-Indische Compagnie—Chartered West India Company)." Under the base of the arms were the words: "Sigillum Amstellodamensis in Novo Belgio,"—the Seal of Amsterdam in New

Belgium (i e. New Netherland)—the whole surrounded by a wreath of laurel.

After Stuyvesant's return from his voyage, and while he was engaged in the task of subjugating the Swedes on the Delaware, in 1655 the Indian trouble so long quiescent broke out again. It seems that van Dyck, the ex-schout, shot a squaw whom he caught stealing peaches in his orchard near the corner of the present Rector Street and Broadway. A party of 1900 savages forthwith took advantage of the director general's absence with the soldiers to beach their canoes at Manhattan very early one morning in September, and broke into several houses on the pretense of searching for Indian enemies. The members of the provincial council, the town magistrates, and other men of prominence hurried to the fort, and parleyed with the sachems, trying to induce them to leave. This they pretended to do, but wreaked their vengeance on van Dyck and another burgher before the citizen guard and the handful of soldiers at the fort could drive them from the island. The savages then proceeded to slaughter and pillage pretty much at their pleasure in the neighborhood of

The Municipality

Manhattan, and prowled around the northern part of the island itself, committing outrages on all who fell in their way. A messenger, thereupon, was hurriedly dispatched to recall Stuyvesant. Comprehending the situation in a moment, he sent off detachments of soldiers to the neighboring settlements; detained for military service able-bodied persons who were about to sail for Europe, cutting short their objections with a curt "possess your souls in patience"; and forbade anyone to leave the town limits without special permission. Fortunately, however, New Amsterdam escaped the horrors of another Indian war. Thanks to the conciliatory methods of the governor, the savages were pacified and their captives ransomed by persuasion and presents, rather than by a resort to the strenuous policy of his predecessor, Kieft.

Stuyvesant now seized the auspicious moment to impress the citizens of New Amsterdam with the necessity of improving the fortifications by having boards nailed along the top of the palisades, so as to prevent the savages from "overloopen" or scaling them. The burghers agreed that the funds for the purpose should be raised by special assessment. But since any form of direct taxation was unpopular, the assessment was to be called a voluntary contribution, because not based on a formal valuation of property. The government, therefore, called upon each burgher to give "according to his state, condition and good will," which circumstances the officials determined in accordance with a rough estimate made in advance. Less than half of the usual taxpayers hastened to avail themselves of such an opportunity to combine patriotism with generosity, as these qualities were rated by burgomasters and schepens. Some ventured to disagree with the official ideas about "state, condition and good will," whereupon their contributions as offered were promptly increased. Others were taxed formally since they "always resorted to one excuse or another." And forcible measures were employed in the case of "disaffected and malevolent" persons, to whom, it would seem, patriotism was not synonymous with purse.

The comparative success of the expedient caused Stuyvesant to suggest to the council the advisability of a general increase in taxation, so

The Municipality

as to reimburse the provincial government for its expenditure on ransoms to the Indians. In his judgment the luxury and high wages then prevailing did not argue an inability to contribute for the public service, but rather a "malevolent unwillingness arising from an imaginary liberty in a new and, as some pretend, a free, country." The council, more amenable to popular opinion, agreed only to an increase in the excise.

Early in 1656 the burgomasters and schepens made another trial at what they had often attempted before. They asked Stuyvesant why other communities in the province enjoyed the privilege of electing their officers, and not New Amsterdam, its capital? The director general replied that this very circumstance explained the denial of the privilege. Such a right, he said, had been granted only because the places in question lay at some distance from the seat of government. He promised, however, that he would vest New Amsterdam with the privilege desired, on condition that the election of magistrates should always be subject to the ratification of the provincial government, that only persons well qualified and agreeable to the director general and the council should be chosen, and that some members of the council should be present when the magistrates actually in office nominated their successors. Yet after the conditions had been accepted, Stuyvesant objected to the choice of the incumbents on the ground of personal distrust, and hence continued the practice of appointing the burgomasters and schepens directly.

Not disheartened by their defeat, the town fathers made further efforts on behalf of municipal rights. Stuyvesant's favorite, van Tienhoven, having been superseded as schout by Nicasius de Sille, they requested the governor to appoint a local schout from among the "intelligent and expert" citizens—that is, of course, if the town itself were not permitted to choose the officer. Stuyvesant resolutely declined thus to weaken the control of the provincial government. On the other hand, he met the wishes of the magistrates by authorizing the schout to enforce the judgments of the municipal court in its own name, by extending the criminal jurisdiction of that body and by allowing town officers to collect fees for recording public docu-

The Municipality

ments. He even created the office of town treasurer to be held by an ex-burgomaster. Since the accounts of this officer were subject to audit by the provincial authorities, Stuyvesant occasionally warned the town government that, unless it kept its accounts straighter, he would be forced to resume management of the municipal revenue-books.

In the firm belief that the concessions that he had just made ought to be followed by a suitable financial response, the director general called upon the town government to pay the arrears of its contributions toward the repair of the fortifications. Evasive promises, complaints about hard times, and a refreshing petition for aid from the Company's own revenues were not what he had expected. He continued, therefore, to exert pressure in the hope of seeing some definite action taken, though to little result.

Municipal individualism having appeared so often in political form, it was now to assume a social guise. The burghers of old Amsterdam, it seems, had recently divided themselves into two classes—"great and small," financial, not physical, considerations fixing the distinction.

The Story *of* New Amsterdam

All citizens who paid to the city 500 guilders enjoyed the title of "Great Burghers," a monopoly of the public offices, and other especial privileges. "Small Burghers" were those who paid 50 guilders for the honor, thereby insuring their right to do business. Desirous of patterning the social structure of New Amsterdam after this model, of safeguarding the town's trade against foreign competition, and, incidentally, of replenishing the municipal treasury, in 1657 the burgomasters and schepens decided to establish there the system of the "burgher-right."

Much democratic criticism was vented later upon this creation of a municipal aristocracy based on wealth alone. In fact it had no extraordinary consequences either political or social. It was a police measure and sprang from an economic motive. The people of New Amsterdam disliked, and very naturally, the itinerant traders who brought to the town nothing of much account while they often carried its money away. Already had it been provided by law that peddlers of the sort should keep "fire and light"—that is, have a reasonably permanent place of business—in the town. Now, since the

The Municipality

number of these undesirable persons showed a tendency to increase, the burgomasters and schepens petitioned Stuyvesant that, in consideration of the burdens the citizens had to bear, and of the loyalty they had always exhibited, they should be allowed to enjoy the close citizenship of the "burgher-right." Regarding the privilege as one of the most important in a well-governed town, they asked the director general to restrict the right of carrying on business in New Amsterdam to such as held the distinction.

In response to this appeal the provincial government decreed that, before attempting to sell their goods, traders must "set up and keep an open store within the gates and walls" of New Amsterdam, and secure from the burgomasters and schepens as well the common or small "burgher-right," for which they would have to pay the town 20 guilders. The body of small burghers, also, should include all freemen who had resided in the town a year and six weeks, all who had married or might marry the daughters of burghers, all who did business regularly in the town, and all the salaried officers of the Dutch West India Company. "In conformity to the

The Story of New Amsterdam

laudable custom of the city of Amsterdam in Europe," there should be established a great "burgher-right," for the enjoyment of which one must pay New Amsterdam 50 guilders. In addition to the business privilege as such, the burghers of this class alone should be eligible to municipal office, be exempt for a year and six weeks from watches and military expeditions, and be free from arrest by order of any inferior court.

Twenty "great burghers" were forthwith enrolled. Among them were the director general, the councillors, the military officers, the municipal authorities, and one woman, Mrs. Cornelius van Tienhoven, whose husband had recently left for parts unknown. The "small burghers" numbered 216, out of a population of about 1000. The inability of the existing body of "great burghers" to fill the municipal offices without absolutely monopolizing them soon became so apparent that, in the year following the establishment of the institution, the director general found it necessary to dilute this exclusive and somewhat unpopular class by adding eight names to its roll. The "small burghers," on the contrary, induced the governor, in 1661, to tighten

The Municipality

their monopoly by expelling any member who absented himself from New Amsterdam for four months without holding "fire and light" there.

With the eligibility to municipal office so narrowly restricted, Stuyvesant had little to fear from encroachments upon the provincial administration, or from undue manifestations of democratic sentiment. He knew, also, that the proceeds from the fees for the enjoyment of the "burgher-right" were to be used largely for military purposes. Accordingly, it is not strange that, when in 1658 the burgomasters and schepens applied once more for leave to nominate a double number of persons out of whom the director general should choose the incumbents for the places to be vacated, Stuyvesant should have consented. Thereafter the town was to possess some right in determining the selection of burgomasters and schepens, limited and far from popular though the privilege might be.

The governor went even farther. He agreed finally to the separation of the office of town schout from that of provincial schout; but he retained the prerogative of appointment in both cases. Thereupon the magistrates of New Amsterdam declined to recognize the new schout, Resolved Waldron by name, and turned for aid and comfort to Brooklyn. Here they found one Pieter Tonneman, an ex-schout and a wily man withal, by whose assistance they managed to circumvent the director general. This Brooklynite they sent to Holland with a petition to the Company for his appointment as town schout. In April, 1660, he returned triumphantly bearing his commission, and Stuyvesant had ruefully to acknowledge that he had been vanquished. So far as the customs of the seventeenth century would allow, the struggle for municipal rights had been fought and won.

CHAPTER V

THE CITY TO-BE

IN tracing the fortunes of the community on Manhattan from its establishment as a trading station to the attainment of its rights as a municipality, two main lines of growth have been visible. Of these, one concerned the efforts to distinguish the town of New Amsterdam as clearly as might be from the province of New Netherland, and the other had to do with the promotion of moral, intellectual and material progress. Local self-improvement and local self-government, indeed, continued throughout to dominate the history of the town so long as the Dutch rule lasted.

Before taking up for consideration the further circumstances under which New Amsterdam secured its distinctive growth, it might be well to glance for a moment at its blood, bone and sinew—the finances, anticipating to some extent facts that will appear later. As a whole the financial system of New Amsterdam resembled that of the average Dutch town, modified of course by its size and local situation, and by its dependence upon the Company. Strictly speaking there was no direct taxation. Even when sums were specially levied for the support of the fire and police departments, they rested on the foundation of immediate payment for service, and fell upon individual houses, chimneys, fireplaces and the like. Certain revenues came from fees, duties and other indirect forms of taxation. Among them were an excise on the brewing and sale of liquors, an excise on the slaughtering of cattle, dues from grocers, fees for stamping weights and measures, fees for surveying land, the proceeds from the disposal of lands owned by the town, the tax on houses and their "appurtenances," and the fees from the "burgher-right." All of the revenues, the right to collect which had been obtained from the provincial government at one time or another, resembled those common to European towns of a fairly advanced type. The levying of special assessments for local improvements, however, was a product

The City To-be

of the new world and its conditions. This took the form of compelling a person to make certain improvements on or near his property for the public good and at his own expense; otherwise the town would do it for him and then charge him proportionately for the outlay. The expenditure of the municipality consisted mainly in the payment of salaries to officials, and in defraying the cost of constructing wooden ramparts and of repairing the walls, the town hall and other public structures. Yet in spite of the various sources of revenue which the town had managed to worry out of the provincial government, and regardless of the fact that the Company itself had been compelled to pay a considerable part of the cost of the fortifications, which it had hoped to impose upon the town, the municipal treasury of New Amsterdam, like that of its successor, New York, often reached the limit of indebtedness.

The most important aspect of municipal development on Manhattan was the moral and religious. Director General Stuyvesant and his provincial advisers, it would seem, accepted absolutely the principle pervading an utterance of

The Story of New Amsterdam

the Reverend Cotton Mather: "If worship be lawful, the compelling to come to it compelleth not to sin, but the sin is in the will that needs to be forced to Christian duty." This principle the provincial government was disposed to apply rather more strictly than was the case with the town fathers of New Amsterdam. Stuyvesant's own interest in the religious welfare of the community became all the more personal when he agreed to pay part of the salary of Domine Selyns, the minister at Brooklyn, on condition that the domine preach on Sunday afternoons in the little chapel which the director general built on his "bouwerie," and which stood on the site of the present St. Mark's Church. Here were assembled in due season all of the members of the Stuyvesant family, the fifty negro slaves and the various white servants in his employ, and a number of religiously inclined people from the town as well.

Up to this time a fair degree of religious toleration had prevailed in New Amsterdam. Whether or not the attitude was due to the small and unobtrusive body of dissenters from the official faith—the Calvinistic Dutch Re-

The City To-be

formed—the fact remains that not until 1654 did anything serious occur to change so wise a policy. In that year the Lutherans ventured to ask permission to worship by themselves. The director general declined to grant it, on the ground that other sects, like Anabaptists, English Independents and their kind, would request the same privilege. Instead, he heeded the Company's advice to "use all moderate exertions" to attract Lutherans to Calvinism. What constituted "moderate exertions" from the official standpoint is illustrated by a proclamation of the governor and council in 1656. It recited that, "whereas . . . conventicles and meetings are held . . . in which some unqualified persons have assumed unto themselves the office of teaching, announcing and declaring God's Holy Word without being called . . . thereunto by authority either of Church or State . . . and because from such manner of gatherings divers mischiefs, heresies and schisms are to be expected, the governor and the council absolutely prohibit all unlawful conventicles of that character." In no respect, however, was this to affect purely private worship at home.

The Story of New Amsterdam

When the Lutherans complained against what they regarded as sheer intolerance, the Company wrote to Stuyvesant: "We would fain not have seen your Worship's hand set to the placard against the Lutherans, nor have heard that you oppressed them. . . . It has always been our intention to let them enjoy all calmness and tranquillity. Wherefore, you will not hereafter publish any similar placards without our previous consent, but allow all the free exercise of their religion in their own houses." The Company, of course, did not perceive that instructions of this sort might be interpreted so as to authorize assemblies for public worship if held in private houses—a view that the orthodox director general would not willingly entertain. Accordingly, in 1657, when the Reverend Ernest Goetwater arrived to take charge of the Lutheran community, Stuyvesant, hearkening to the objections of the two Calvinist clergymen, Megapolensis and Drisius, who were something of heresy-hunters, forbade him to hold any meeting or to perform any religious function whatever. In this action the Company upheld the governor, but observed that it "might have been done in

The City To-be

a more gentle way." Realizing, furthermore, that the strenuous qualities of the director general displayed themselves in religious as well as in secular concerns, it enjoined him to moderate measures in order that "those of other persuasions may not be frightened away through such a preciseness in the public Reformed Church . . . but by attending its services may be attracted and gained." It added significantly that, if it sent any more clergymen, they would be persons "not tainted with any needless preciseness, which is rather prone to create schisms than . . . adapted to edify the flock."

Denials of religious toleration did not stop with the Lutherans. In August, 1657, a number of Quakers, including several who had recently been expelled from Boston, arrived at New Amsterdam. Two of the women of the party soon began to preach in the streets, "pretending to be divinely inspired . . . and made a terrible hue and cry, crying woe! woe! to the crown of pride and the drunkards of Ephraim! Two woes past and the third coming, except ye repent." They also appear to have entered the church, making a great disturbance. Utterances of this kind Stuyvesant doubtless believed inspired—though not from above; for that reason he promptly ordered the Quakers out of the province. One of the men, however, was condemned to labor two years at a wheelbarrow alongside of a negro convict, or pay a fine of 600 guilders. After having been chained to the wheelbarrow and ordered to work he refused, whereupon he was beaten by the negro with a tarred rope till he fell unconscious. Even worse tortures were applied in the town hall prison without extorting from him any repentance until Mrs. Bayard, the director general's sister, interceded on his behalf. Stuyvesant then expelled him from the province also.

Following these measures came a proclamation announcing that the entertainment of a Quaker would be visited with a heavy fine, half of which was to go to the informer, and that vessels bringing Quakers to New Amsterdam would be liable to confiscation. Since the wrath of the Almighty had become manifest in "permitting . . . the spirit of error to scatter its injurious poison . . . in spiritual matters . . . raising up and propagating a new, unheard of, abominable heresy called Quakers seeking to seduce many," the director general and the council appointed a day of fasting, prayer and thanksgiving, so as to ward off any other signs of divine displeasure. On that day, while the religious observances were in progress, "all exercises and amusements, tennis, ball-playing, hunting, fishing, sailing; also all unlawful plays, such as gaming, dice-playing, drunkenness and the like" were prohibited on pain of "arbitrary punishment and correction," i. e. whipping at the post in front of the town hall. The same punishment Stuyvesant ordered some years later to be inflicted upon persons who had participated more than twice in the public exercise of any religion, except the Reformed, in "houses, barns, ships, woods, or fields."

So drastic a policy did not meet with the approval of the Company. "Although it is our cordial desire," wrote that body to Stuyvesant, "that . . . sectarians may not be found there, yet as the contrary seems to be the fact, we doubt very much whether rigorous proceeding against them ought not to be discontinued; unless, indeed, you intend to check and destroy your population, which in the youth of your existence ought rather to be encouraged by all possible means. Wherefore, it is our opinion that some connivance is useful, and that at least the consciences of men ought to remain free and unshackled. Let everyone remain free as long as he is modest, moderate, his political conduct irreproachable, and as long as he does not offend others or oppose the government." The admonition proved to be effective, and no more religious persecution darkened New Amsterdam or its vicinity.

Aside from "exercises and amusements" that violated the laws of public worship, Stuyvesant in general did not eye with favor any sports and games that offended his sense of propriety. For this reason he forbade certain farmers' servants to "ride the goose on the feast of Bacchus at Shrovetide." "It is altogether unprofitable, unnecessary, and censurable," he declared, "for subjects and neighbors to celebrate such pagan and popish feasts, and to practice such evil customs in this country, even though they may be tolerated and looked at through the fingers in some places in the Fatherland." The pastime was in fact a cruel one. It consisted of greasing a live

The City To-be

goose, hanging it up, and while riding swiftly by, endeavoring to catch the bird by the head. When, however, the director general punished some persons for disregarding his command, the burgomasters and schepens complained that his action, without their knowledge and consent, had exceeded his authority within the town limits. The remonstrance evoked the sarcastic rejoinder: "as if we can issue no order or forbid no rabble to celebrate the feast of Bacchus without the advice, knowledge and consent of burgomasters and schepens, much less have power to correct such persons that transgress the Christian and holy commandment, without the cognizance and consent of a little court of justice." Stuyvesant, of course, did not care whether the protest of the burgomasters and schepens arose from liberal views about holiday diversions or from a jealous regard for the protection of the town against the encroachments of the provincial government; he was simply determined to suppress all forms of frivolity that differed from his canons of correct deportment. Indeed he went still further in his proclamation of December, 1655. "Whereas," it ran, "experience has

The Story *of* New Amsterdam

manifested and shown that on New Years and May days much drunkenness and other irregularities are committed, besides other sorrowful accidents, such as woundings, frequently arising therefrom by firing, May-planting and carousing, in addition to the unnecessary waste of powder; to prevent which ... the Director General and Council expressly forbid ... within this province ... on New Years or May days any firing of guns, or any planting of May poles or any beating of drums or any treating with brandy, wine or beer." Thereafter the working off of surplus enthusiasm became increasingly difficult.

Despite enactments to the contrary, the imbibing of "hot and rebellious" liquors, as well as of less noxious ones, at forbidden times, especially on Sunday, was persisted in to such an extent that, in 1656, the director general and the council resolved to check the practice by a comprehensive ordinance that gives further insight into the amusements of the sporting element in New Amsterdam. Not only were ordinary occupations to be laid aside on the Lord's Day, but also "any lower or unlawful exercises or games,

The City To-be

drunkenness, frequenting taverns or grog-shops, dancing, card-playing, back-gammon, tennis, ball-playing, bowling, rolling nine-pins, racing with boats, cars or wagons before, during or between divine service" were strictly forbidden. "More especially," ran the ordinance, "no tavern-keepers or tapsters shall allow any clubs to sit during, before or between the sermons," or on days other than Sunday "after the setting of the night watch or ringing of the bell"; or "tap, present, give or sell directly or indirectly" liquors to any person, under the penalties of fines upon the guests and upon the tapster, both for the offence and for each one of such guests. The prohibition thus to be regaled at unseasonable times, however, did not apply to persons "attending by order and with consent of magistrates to public business."

In prosecuting violations of the law against the sale of liquor on Sunday it was relatively as difficult then as it was in later centuries to obtain evidence sufficient for conviction. On one occasion Resolved Waldron, the schout, haled Solomon La Chair, the bellicose notary, before the municipal court on the charge of breaking the law in this respect. He declared that he had gone to La Chair's house "before the preaching and found a man in the house and a glass with brandy in it; also returning in the afternoon he found a glass with beer or something else, he knows not what, in it." When, also, he undertook to chide the defendant for desecrating the Sabbath he was promptly called a rascal. On his own behalf La Chair asserted that "he had been on the watch, and coming home in the morning he tapped a little drop for himself of which some remained in the glass, and that he thereupon went to sleep. Meanwhile people came into the house but did not tap; and in the afternoon some beer remained in the glass. . . . Denying to have ill-treated the officer, but said 'Come, see here what the house contains.'" The "man in the house," Jan Los by name, admitted that the defendant "gave him a little sup," but the schout "cannot say that he had drank it." The schout then declared that Los was present when La Chair dubbed him a rascal, to which Los "being asked, answers he did not hear but says he heard talk, but knows not what." The municipal court thereupon dismissed the com-

The City To-be

plaint on the ground that prosecution had been unable to produce "any proper proof."

It has already been observed that Resolved Waldron, as the director general's appointee to the office of town schout, stood in no great favor with the town magistrates; hence it is not altogether surprising that his successor, Pieter Tonneman, the wily man from Brooklyn, and the town's own chosen schout, should have secured a conviction on about the same amount of evidence. Before the court of burgomasters and schepens he stated that he had fined the wife of Andreas Rees "because there were nine-pins at her house last Sunday during preaching and the can and glass stood on the table." In response Rees declared "that he was not at home, but on the watch, and that there were no nine-pins at his house or . . . drinking . . . during the preaching." His wife also contended "that there were no nine-pins or drinking at her house, saying that some came to her house who said that church was out, and that one had a pin and the other a bowl in the hand, but they did not play." In rebuttal the schout asserted that the defendant's wife had said "she did not know that church was out," and, "trying to corrupt his official integrity in an artful manner," had offered to "compound with him!" The defendant, accordingly, was condemned by the court to pay a fine of six guilders.

A more interesting attempt to safeguard the morality of New Amsterdam is found in an ordinance that provided virtually for the abolition of long engagements! Since betrothed persons, it seems, had postponed their marriage until a long time after the banns had been published, which conduct was "directly in contravention of the . . . excellent order and practice of our Fatherland," all such persons in future would have to marry within a month after their engagement had been announced, unless they could give a good excuse to the contrary. The consternation thereby awakened among prospective husbands, and the utter chaos in arrangements for trousseaux thereby caused among prospective brides did not affect this rigid decree, so long as the Dutch rulers presided over the destinies of New Amsterdam.

In a similar connection it will be remembered that, when the burgomasters and schepens ap-

The City To-be

plied to Stuyvesant for the privilege of choosing orphan-masters, they had been ordered to leave the care of widows and orphans to the deacons. But persistent endeavor in this respect, rather than any lack of confidence in the deacons, eventually obtained for the town magistrates the right to appoint, not only orphan-masters, but churchwardens as well. About the same time, in 1658, solicitude on the part of the Company's surgeon for the helpless and afflicted led to the establishment of the first hospital on Manhattan. Here the patients were to be taken care of by a faithful person who should supply them with food, fire and light, while the doctors furnished the medicine, and presumably the barbers, the surgery! In this year, also, the first coroner's inquest in New Amsterdam appears to have been held.

Passing now from morals to intellect, it appears that, after the public school had taken up its quarters in the town hall in spite of the grumblings of the loungers, the portly size of these persons, and the presence of sundry huge sacks of salt stored in the building seriously limited the amount of space available for official uses. Accordingly the burgomasters and schepens ordered both of the encumbrances to be removed, so that the hall "be not wholly ruined by the salt nor occupied by the lodgers." So large, indeed, became the attendance at the school that, in May, 1655, Willem Veestens, the teacher, had to transfer his flock to a building on Pearl Street. His successor in the post was one Harmanus van Hoboocken, who was superseded in turn by Evert Pietersen at a salary of $14.50 a month and $50 allowance for board a year.

By this time the magistrates of New Amsterdam had become convinced of the necessity for higher education. In 1658 they wrote to the Company as follows: "Laying before your Honors the great augmentation of the youth in this . . . place which yearly increases more and more, and finds itself now very numerous; and though many of them can read and write, the burghers and inhabitants are nevertheless inclined to have their children instructed in the most useful languages, the chief of which is the Latin tongue; and as there are no means to do so here . . . we shall therefore . . . trouble your

The City To-be

Honors and humbly request that you would be pleased to send us a suitable person for master of a Latin school . . . hoping that it may finally attain to an academy whereby this place arriving at great splendor from your Honors shall have the reward and praise. . . . On your Honors sending us a schoolmaster we shall endeavor to have constructed a suitable place for the school." To this request the Company readily acceded, and a gentleman named Alexander Carolus Curtius, the sound of whose name might reasonably argue a knowledge of the Latin tongue, came in 1659 to administer learning in the first high school established on Manhattan, and that for boys only. The capacity of girls for absorbing Latin was not then appreciated. From the public school they were graduated forthwith into the kitchen and the sewing-room, where they might indulge their linguistic talents in other directions.

Though Alexander Carolus Curtius may have had a good knowledge of dead languages, he did not know much about live boys, whose wish to learn that all Gaul was divided into three parts did not equal their desire to ascertain into how many parts they could tear one another's clothes. Accordingly, since the parents of his pupils would not permit him to leave any impressions on their offspring other than mental ones, he failed to associate Roman discipline with a Latin education. This fact, coupled with his claim as a professor to exemption from taxes—a claim which the magistrates promptly overruled—led to his supersession in 1662 by one Aegidius Luyck, whose last name, if less Romanic than that of his predecessor, had certainly a more auspicious sound to it. In point of fact, Aegidius Luyck made such a reputation for his discipline and his Latin that pupils flocked to the school from various parts of the province and even from Virginia.

Reverting once more to the matter of the observance of Sunday, the accounts already given of its regulation by law, in accordance with the Calvinistic standards of the seventeenth century, show that it occupied an important place among public improvements in the city to-be. The impulse in this direction appears to have emanated more from the strict piety of Director General Stuyvesant than from the conscientious scruples

The City To-be

of burgomasters and schepens. For example, in 1663, the town magistrates were reminded by the director general that previous ordinances on the subject had been disregarded by some persons who had misconstrued their terms to mean the observance of only half the Sabbath. In order, therefore, to remove false impressions or interpretations on this score, the magistrates themselves proclaimed the order of the governor and council that henceforth not only a part but the whole of the Sabbath should be kept sacred. Customary labor, and in particular the gathering of social clubs, were absolutely forbidden. Under the same prohibition were placed all "unusual exercises such as games, boat, cart or wagon racing, fishing, fowling, running, sailing, nutting or picking strawberries, trafficking with Indians . . . all dissolute . . . plays, riots, and calling children out to the streets and highways." As penalties for the first offence the forfeiture of the upper garment or a fine of six guilders was prescribed, these penalties increasing to corporal punishment in case of repetition.

Though agreeing with Stuyvesant and the council that an enactment of this sort was desirable, in their actual judgments the burgomasters and schepens suitably tempered its severity. On one occasion the schout prosecuted a man before the municipal court for having worked at his cart on Sunday. In his own defense the culprit said that he "merely took a pin out of his cart through fear that . . . boys would otherwise ride" it to pieces. Another individual was brought to book for having cut wood on Sunday to keep his children warm, and still another pleaded guilty to having cut a stick as a plaything for his little boy. In all these cases the magistrates dismissed the offenders with a simple reprimand.

In addition to the regulation of morals and the encouragement of education, salutary measures were adopted to safeguard the persons and property of the citizens, by calling into existence the Dutch forerunners of the metropolitan fire and police departments. Since the wooden houses with their thatched roofs and wooden chimneys were too near equally inflammable haystacks, in 1657 the town authorities ordered the latter to be moved to a safe distance. In the following year they levied a tax of one guilder on

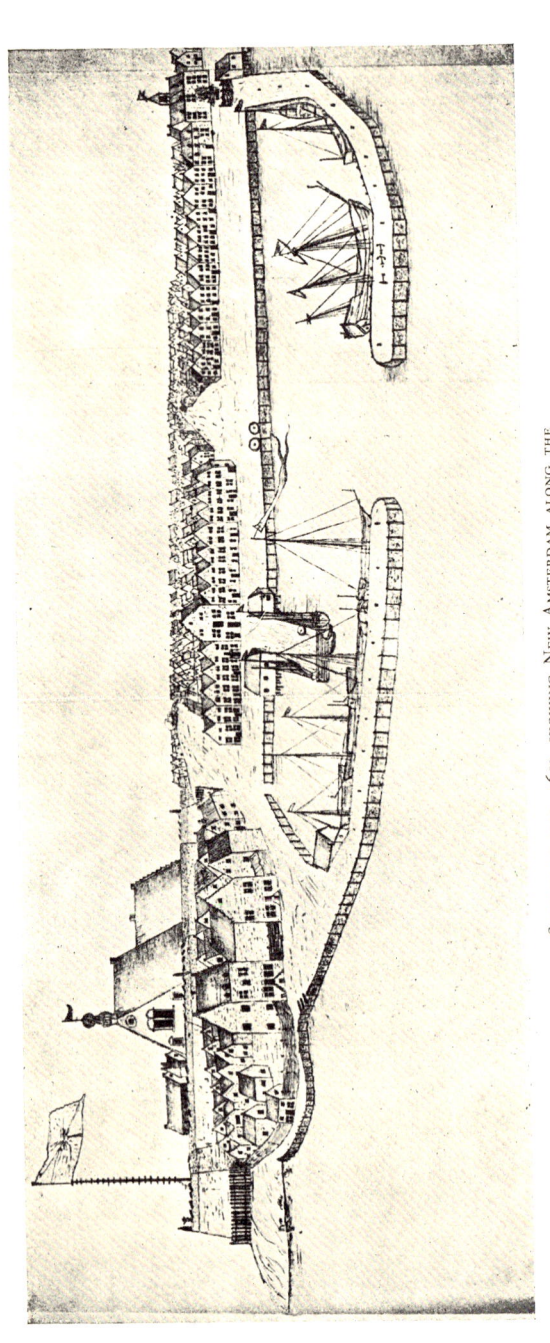

Section of map, 1679, showing New Amsterdam along the East River from the fort to the town hall.
"Journal of Jasper Danckaerts," *Long Island Historical Society Memoirs*, I.

The City To-be

each chimney, from the proceeds of which tax hooks and ladders and leather fire-buckets were to be purchased. So as to avoid the delay and difficulty incident to the importation of the buckets from the Netherlands, the magistrates resolved to patronize home industry, and accordingly made a contract with the shoemakers of New Amsterdam to supply the town with a suitable number. The buckets were placed at the corners of the streets, in public buildings, and in other places convenient of access. Fifty of them were deposited in the town hall at Coenties Slip, twelve in a tavern near the corner of Broad and Pearl Streets, and a like number in a private house in the "Smit's Vly." This apparatus, and the supervision of the two fire-wardens, constituted the first fire department on Manhattan. Some years later, when it became known that certain rich people had a number of fire-places connected with the same chimney, thus causing the incidence of taxation to fall unequally, the town government ordered the assessment to be levied upon each fire-place instead.

More or less as an adjunct to the fire department, the project of forming a "rattle watch," or regular police force, was mooted in 1654, as a substitute for the volunteer citizen's night watch; or in the words of the record: "by consideration of the small accommodation and convenience for the citizen's watch, and likewise because of the great cost of fire and light for the same, making it burdensome upon the citizens to sustain them during the winter." At this time, however, no one seemed inclined to assume the duty of springing a rattle to frighten off the midnight marauder, of detecting the presence of fire, or of calling out the hours and of assuring the Dutchmen who sonorously slept them away that all was well. Not until 1658 did the magistrates feel emboldened to issue an ordinance governing the organization and activity of the first police force established on Manhattan. It was composed of a captain and eight men who were to be on duty from nine o'clock in the evening till drum-beat, approximately six o'clock in the morning. The salary attached to the office of policeman was to be eighteen guilders a month, certain allowances for candles, and several hundred sticks of fire-wood. For the support of the force the captain was authorized to

The City To-be

collect fifteen stivers a month from each household.

A close inspection of the rules and regulations shows that the management of policemen was not an easy task. Fines were imposed for tardiness in arriving at the "usual hour, to wit, before bell ring"; for not coming in person to serve on the watch, or if detained for good cause, not sending a substitute; for appearing drunk on duty; for indulging in any "opposition or insolence . . . within the square of the Town Hall," or in going the rounds; for sleeping or other negligence on post; for failure to catch thieves; and for "lying still" when people called "Watch! Watch!" Subject to like penalties were such further evidences of misconduct as swearing or fighting while on duty, unwillingness "to go around or in any way lose a turn," and being off post without leave. On the other hand fines were inflicted on persons who challenged any member of the watch "to come with him to fight," or threatened a policeman "to beat him in the morning," when the watch was dismissed. The record then adds: "Whatever any of the watch shall get from any of the prisoners,

The Story of New Amsterdam

whether lock-up money, present or other fee, which those of the watch shall receive by consent of the burgomasters ... shall be brought into the hands of the captain for the benefit of the fellow watchmen and shall be there preserved until it be divided around." The proceeds from fines, also, were to be divided four times a year among the members of the watch, "without their holding any drinking meeting thereupon or keeping any club."

Great as the inducements for service appear to have been, it was not until January, 1661, that the police department of New Amsterdam reached final organization. Its members were Captain Lodowyck Pos and Patrolmen Jan Cornelisen van Vlensburgh, Hendrick Hendrickzen van Doesburgh, Cornelis Hendricksen, Andries Andriesen, Cornelis Barensen, Pieter Jansen van de Lange Straat, Pieter Jansen Werckendam and Mattys Muller—altogether a fairly solid Dutch phalanx.

Closely associated with this care for the protection of person and property was that shown by the magistrates in fostering the business interests of New Amsterdam. The appointment, in

The City To-be

1655, of a high constable or town marshal to enforce judicial proceedings in civil cases tended to make business activities more secure. To remedy the lack of a suitable currency, the burgomasters and schepens petitioned the Company to authorize the establishment of a mint for the coinage of silver, and the conversion of sewant into an article of trade, which would promote the purchase of furs from the Indians. Perceiving no especial advantage in the proposal, the Company declined to consider it. On the other hand, business was aided by the appointment, in 1656, of an official broker who served the Dutch and English merchants in their transactions, and who received a commission on sales. The merchants met on 'change Friday morning near the corner of the present Bridge and Broad Streets—a centre of trade that has not greatly shifted in more than two centuries and a half.

Hard by this first exchange on Manhattan lay the market-place, on the corner of Broad and Pearl Streets, to which on Saturday mornings the country folk brought their produce and where they placed their wagons—much to the annoyance of one prominent citizen, Allard Anthony,

The Story *of* New Amsterdam

whose wife and daughters disliked the proximity of the market to their own house. As a supplement to this emporium the town magistrates erected a meat-market, and licensed official butchers. Another measure that protected the pocket as well as the health of the citizens was the appointment of two inspectors of baking, who were to take care "that the bread within the jurisdiction of this town be baked of good material and due weight, and as it comes from the mill unmixed or with other stuff amongst it." But as the price of bread fixed at the same time proved unprofitable, on petition of the bakers, the burgomasters and schepens agreed to raise the price to twenty-six stivers for an eight pound loaf of wheat, and to twenty-two stivers for a loaf of rye.

Commercial business, no less than mercantile, had its share of attention also. Cargoes had been landed hitherto in scows at the wharf on the line of the present Moore Street, and jutting out from Pearl, or they had been discharged directly from vessels of small draught that came up the creek running through the middle of Broad Street as far as Exchange Place. The

The City To-be

growth of shipping soon made an enlargement of the wharf at Moore Street necessary, and in 1658 led to the erection of a dock near the corner of Bridge and Broad Streets where the exchange was held. These structures, for the use of which the city charged so much per "last" or double ton, were the scant beginnings of the vast system of docks and wharves that now line the river front of New York.

One of the activities along the East River side of New Amsterdam that needed regulation was the ferry from Peck Slip to Brooklyn. So much "daily confusion" and, incidentally, competition, had arisen among the ferrymen on Manhattan, that sometimes people had to wait "whole days before they could obtain a passage, and then not without danger, and at an exorbitant price." To cope with this situation, the director general and the council ordered that no person should conduct a ferry without a license, and that the ferrymen should always keep "proper servants, boats and lodges" on both sides of the river. In summer the passengers should be accommodated from five o'clock A. M. to eight o'clock P. M., and in winter, from seven o'clock A. M. to five o'clock P. M., provided that the windmill "hath not taken in its sail," this being supposedly an infallible barometer that indicated the approach of bad weather. On the other hand, no one need be taken across before the payment of ferriage, except the director general, the members of the council and other official persons, who should be allowed to ride free.

The control of this ferry and the management of the public weigh-scales often aroused controversy between the provincial and the town authorities. The governor had always maintained that the proceeds from the ferry and the fees exacted for the public weighing of goods were perquisites belonging to the Company alone. Beset, however, by the constant protests and importunities of the burgomasters and schepens, Stuyvesant and the council at length agreed, in 1658, to allow one-fourth of the revenue to be paid into the municipal treasury—a concession that was promptly annulled by the Company. The matter came up again in 1663. On account of trouble with the Indians at Esopus (Kingston), the director general requested the town to maintain a military force that would be able to aid

CORNELIUS STEENWIJCK, SOMETIME SCHEPEN OF NEW AMSTERDAM, AND MAYOR OF NEW YORK, 1668-1670. NOTE THE VIEW OF NEW AMSTERDAM BELOW

From the original painting in the possession of the New York Historical Society

The City To-be

other settlements in time of distress. The magistrates of New Amsterdam readily consented to enroll twenty or twenty-five men and provide suitably for their support, on condition that the town might raise the necessary money by a loan based upon the security of the funds accruing from the weigh-scales and the ferry. The approach of the crisis of 1664 prevented any realization of this plan.

The wisdom of bettering the appearance and the facilities of a city to-be that, in 1655, boasted a census of 120 houses and 1000 inhabitants, so impressed the burgomasters and schepens that in November of that year they resolved to have the town properly surveyed for the location of lots and the alinement of streets. They accordingly appointed a commission, made up of the two town surveyors, one burgomaster, and one member of the provincial council, to undertake the task. In the following year the commission surveyed the lots and fixed their prices; then laid out seventeen streets and marked them by stakes. So as to preserve the compactness of the town, the magistrates issued an ordinance directing the holders of lots to build on them within a specified time under pain of forfeiture. This decree was read by the crier as usual to the citizens assembled around the "puy" or platform in front of the town hall by the ringing of the bell which the magistrates had recently induced the director general to transfer from the fort to the belfry of this edifice. For some reason the ordinance proved incapable of enforcement; hence the burgomasters and schepens proceeded to lessen the penalty prescribed by merely taxing the vacant lots as such at the owner's valuation, but reserving the right to purchase it, again at the owner's valuation, and grant it to some one else. The tax, of course, ceased as soon as a house had been built on the property.

In 1657 the question of paving the streets came up for discussion. As often is the case with municipal improvements, the idea was suggested by a woman. This was Mrs. Oloff Stevensen van Cortlandt, whose husband's brewery and residence lay on Brouwer, or Brewer, Street between the present Whitehall and Broad Streets. The street in question, it seems, was so dusty that the worthy dame could not keep her house clean, hence she ventilated the subject so vigorously

The City To-be

among her neighbors that they petitioned the burgomasters and schepens to have the thoroughfare paved. The work was assigned to a contractor who laid down a rude paving of cobble stones or the like, whereupon the name of the street was changed to that which it now bears, Stone Street. Since the paving had been undertaken by the town at the request of the property owners, its cost was apportioned among these persons, thereby furnishing one of the first examples of the levy of a special assessment to which allusion has already been made. Before 1661, presumably by a resort to this method of taxation, all of the streets most in use had been paved. The gutters lay in the middle of the street which served as a highway for man and beast alike, since sidewalks there were none.

A similar plan to promote the cause of public improvements is visible in the resolution of the town magistrates about the same time to check the tendency of the banks along the inlet running through the centre of the present Broad Street to cave in, by shoring them up with planks and charging the resultant cost upon the owners of the adjacent property. These individuals, however, did not receive the idea kindly. They denounced the proposed improvement as useless, extravagant and undesirable; but they remarked ingenuously that, if it were to be made at the expense of the town, it would greatly benefit the public at large. The distinction does not seem to have penetrated Stuyvesant, or if it did he evinced no sign, for he had the natural canal widened to sixteen feet, its banks properly strengthened, and the roadway on each side of the stream made twenty-eight feet in breadth, or in all seventy-two feet, which is the average width of Broad Street to-day. When some of the property holders wrathfully declined to pay, Stuyvesant simply locked them up until they cooled off and changed their minds.

The wooden sidings and other betterments along the canal were so useful that in 1660 still further action was taken. A town ordinance of that year, after alluding to the advantages enjoyed by the residents of the immediate neighborhood in having a landing-place without the expense of a dock, prescribed that these favored persons should themselves pave the roadways on both banks of the canal; otherwise the town

The City To-be

would do it at their expense. Moreover, to keep that water highway free from obstructions, the throwing of any rubbish into it was strictly prohibited. When some people were prosecuted for violating the ordinance, they proved to the satisfaction of the magistrates that, since the rubbish they had dumped into the canal was snow, it probably would not interfere very much with navigation, and they were accordingly released.

The preservation of thoroughfares from nuisance, especially that made by roving animals of the domestic sort, had often engaged the attention of the authorities; but the measures hitherto adopted to protect the streets of the town and the walls of the fort also against the destructive undermining of that insidious leveler, the wandering pig, had been so ineffective that the director general and the council ordered the inhabitants in future to put rings through the snouts of all such miscreants. One class of animals, however, obtained favorable consideration, namely, the cows belonging to the burghers of New Amsterdam. Perhaps the possession of the exclusive burgher-right by their owners may have suggested the creation of a kind of bovine

The Story of New Amsterdam

aristocracy as well. At all events, in 1660, a tract of land near the "Collect," or the Fresh Water—the pond about Centre Street—hitherto used as a common for pasturing cattle, was fenced in and reserved for the burgher cows alone. One Gabriel Carpsey was their herdsman, and, like his angelic namesake, he carried a horn which, to pursue the likeness still further, he blew in the morning at the gates of the owners, collected his drove and conducted it along Broadway through Pearl Street and Maiden Lane to its exclusive pasture. In the evening the procession wound slowly homeward from the lea, and Gabriel's trumpet announced the several arrivals at the proper destination.

The wooden siding along the banks of the watery portion of Broad Street, erected at the expense of the vicinage, was not the only structure of the kind. On account of the necessity of protecting the shore in front of the town hall and the houses of the inhabitants along Pearl Street against the inroads of high tides from the East River, the magistrates decided to have planks driven down and a "schoeynge" or sheet-piling thus made. It extended from the foot of Broad

The City To-be

Street to the town hall at Coenties Slip, thence to the "Water-gate" at the corner of Pearl and Wall Streets. The fine dry walk formed in this way was called the "Waal," and is to be distinguished from Wall Street which ran nearly at right angles to it. Along this promenade the young men and maidens of the town were wont to take their evening stroll, "watching the silver moonbeams as they trembled on the calm bosom of the bay, or lit up the sail of some gliding bark, and peradventure interchanging the soft vows of honest affection." The proximity, furthermore, of Director General Stuyvesant's new residence on the corner of State and Whitehall Streets to the promenade of the "Waal" might serve to explain why he too was occasionally to be found among the strollers, though not, however, of the romantic sort just described. His official domicile in the fort had become so dilapidated that, in 1659, he found it necessary to change his quarters. The new house was made out of hewn white stone, a circumstance that gave its name to Whitehall Street. Gardens surrounded the mansion on three sides, and in front the lawn stretched down to the water's edge.

CHAPTER VI

THE PASSING OF NEW AMSTERDAM

THE foregoing study of municipal growth naturally suggests a broad survey of the town's topography on the eve of the passing of New Amsterdam. The actual area, of course, was not very large. The habit of crowding together for various reasons had retarded the process of extension. In particular the barrier formed by Wall Street not only kept Indians and possible enemies from New England out, but also on its northern line kept the town in. At its southern end, moreover, Manhattan is now much broader than it was during the period of the Dutch occupation. Many of the mud flats then in existence have been filled in, and on them streets laid out as, for example, Water Street. A great part of the Battery has been similarly reclaimed from the tides.

From the so-called "Marckvelt" or Market-

The Passing of New Amsterdam

field—the later "plaine" or Bowling Green—in front of the fort, where markets, fairs and festivities were often held, a road to the west of the town ran northward up a rather thinly populated hill. As it was the principal highway from which one could pass into the "Land-gate" at the Western end of Wall Street, it bore the name of the "Heere Straat" or "Main Street," and still retains its prominence as Broadway. From the "Marckvelt" eastward was a thoroughfare known as the "Marckvelt Steegie," the present Marketfield Street, leading to the "Heere Gracht," now Broad Street. The thoroughfare behind Fort Amsterdam, then extending properly from State Street to Whitehall Street, was the oldest and apparently the most populous on the island, and still keeps its Dutch name of Pearl Street, however anglicized the mode of spelling. In the rear of the town hall ran a highway, known to-day by its English equivalent of High Street, from a bridge over the outlet of the Broad Street canal along the East River to the "Water-gate" at the junction of Pearl and Wall Street, where one might leave the town on its eastern side. On High Street were located the residences of the well-to-do folk of New Amsterdam.

From the "Water-gate" the main road crossed the present Roosevelt Street, at that time a stream called the "old kill," by the famous "Kissing Bridge." "Here," says an English clergyman of the eighteenth century, it was "customary before passing beyond to salute the lady who is your companion." On his own behalf he ingenuously admitted that he found the practice "curious, yet not displeasing"! Indeed it seems to have been so much appreciated by the young men of the period, and possibly also by the young women, that at several other bridges on Manhattan, ordinarily free to cross, it became the rule to collect toll of this description. North of the "Kissing Bridge" the road came to a hill so steep that a roundabout way had to be devised. The loop thus made still exists in the form of Chatham Square. North of this in turn lay the "bouwerie" of Director General Stuyvesant, which served as the nucleus of Bowery Village.

Considerably to the northward lay still another settlement which in the twentieth century

The Passing *of* New Amsterdam

has become of prime importance, whatever its standing in the seventeenth may have been. Situated north of a line stretching from the present Central Park West and 112th Street to the East River at 100th Street were broad, moist and fertile meadows called by the Dutch "The Flats." Because of an apparent similarity to their own well-watered lowlands at home, Dutch settlers had established themselves there quite early. So large comparatively did the number become that, in 1658, the director general and the council resolved to promote the progress of agriculture and also to provide a "place of amusement for the burghers of New Amsterdam," by elevating the hamlet to the dignity of a village. The selection of a name gave rise to a small tempest. Every resident Dutchman naturally wanted it to be called after his own native town. The gratification of all these desires would probably have stunted the growth of the village by the mere weight of names, hence Stuyvesant found it expedient to make the choice himself. Having ascertained that none of the settlers had come from Haarlem, he forestalled any sentiment of jealousy by naming the place New

Haarlem. Liberal inducements were offered to newcomers. A good road to facilitate transit between the village and New Amsterdam "on horseback or in a wagon," a ferry to Long Island, the organization of a court, and the appointment of "a good orthodox clergyman" as soon as the village should have a population of twenty-five families, were all promised. Ere long a little tavern rose on the banks of the Harlem River, and became a popular resort for pleasure parties from the city; but just why it should have been christened the "Wedding Place" does not appear.

By 1660 New Haarlem contained the requisite number of families, and was accordingly vested with a separate village government, composed of a deputy schout and three schepens appointed by the magistrates of New Amsterdam out of a double number presented by the retiring board. Subordinate of course to the municipal authorities, the village was destined to reproduce some of the individuality of the parent town, and like it in the course of the centuries has come to spread over a much wider area. Yet in the straw-thatched farmhouses on the flats of New

The Passing of New Amsterdam

Haarlem one may hardly detect the earliest form of the institution known as the "Harlem flat"!

How long before the various outlying communities would have become merged in the parent town may never be known, for the passing of New Amsterdam was at hand. Disquieting rumors from abroad and the rebellious behavior of the English towns under Dutch jurisdiction on Long Island caused Stuyvesant, in February, 1664, to call a joint meeting of the council with the burgomasters and schepens, as was his custom when about to consider matters of great public moment. He asked the advice of the assembled body as to the feasibility of suppressing the insurrection on Long Island, and of fortifying New Amsterdam against possible attacks from England or from the colonists of that country beyond the Connecticut River. With justifiable pride the municipal magistrates declared that the town adorned as it was "with so many noble buildings at the expense of the good and faithful inhabitants . . . that it nearly excels any other place in North America," should be well fortified, and its military force increased, thereby "to instill fear into any envious neighbors." But when the governor asked for contributions to this end, the burgomasters and schepens displayed a spirit of caution which did not reveal any marked degree of loyalty to their mother country.

The attitude of the town fathers of New Amsterdam in this respect is not difficult to understand. The neglect shown by the Dutch West India Company, and even by the Dutch government, and the extent to which the genuine interests of the colonists had been ignored, were responsible for the haggling that ensued over questions of expenditure, the procrastination, and even the indifference as to the outcome, provided only that their lives, property and privileges should be spared. In reply, therefore, to the request of the director general for pecuniary aid, the burgomaster and schepens pleaded poverty, and intimated that the Company, through Stuyvesant as its representative in New Netherland, ought to furnish a few hundred soldiers and pay them from the money it received in customs duties. The governor then asked them to make some arrangement for the erection of defensive palisades. To this the magistrates responded that the Company's negro slaves ought to be employed in cutting and hauling them. As an illustration of their real indifference as to whether England or the Netherlands had possession of New Netherland, the following may be cited from the records: "We are of opinion," said the magistrates, "that the burgher is not bound to dispute whether this be the king of England's soil or their High Mightinesses, but if they (the English) will deprive (us) of our properties, freedoms, and privileges, (we are bound) to resist them with our lives and fortunes." Such a statement must have seemed to a man of Stuyvesant's mold a sordid and pusillanimous, if not indeed a treasonable, performance. But he succeeded in keeping his temper, and proceeded to inquire sarcastically whether the city militia would assume any share whatever in the measures of defence. This query the magistrates answered calmly by remarking that the burgher guard might keep watch by night, but that the Company's soldiers in the fort should mount guard by day.

Eventually the town fathers came to the conclusion that fortifications in the shape of a stone wall ought to be erected on the land side of Manhattan, and palisades also along the shores of both rivers. For this purpose they declared a loan should be raised, on condition that all of the revenues from the excise be turned into the municipal treasury. Under the circumstances the director general had to yield, and he accordingly surrendered the tax for a period of five years within which the debt incurred by the town in raising the loan would have to be paid off. He stipulated, however, that the municipality enlist a volunteer force of 200 men and provide for their maintenance as well as for that of 160 regular soldiers. To these ends the sum of 27,500 guilders was soon raised on the security of town property and the proceeds from the excise.

In their attitude of reluctance, be it said, the burgomasters and schepens did not stand alone. Popular conventions from New Amsterdam and vicinity, summoned by Stuyvesant at their suggestion, to deliberate on the state of the province, displayed much the same spirit. Throughout they declined to vote supplies or to approve the drafting of men until the director general could afford better assurances that the Company

The Passing of New Amsterdam

would perform its share of the common obligations.

Warned that an English expedition had sailed from Portsmouth, presumably with hostile designs against New Netherland, the citizens of New Amsterdam had begun more active measures for defence when a reassuring letter arrived from the Company. Deceived by false information from London, the Company notified the residents of the province that they need apprehend no danger, since King Charles II had dispatched the squadron for the purpose merely of adjusting certain matters in New England and of establishing there the Anglican faith. Stuyvesant accordingly went to Fort Orange (Albany) on business, but he had hardly arrived at his destination when the news that the English vessels had been sighted off the Massachusetts coast caused the council to recall the director general in haste. Realizing now that the situation might become serious the schout, burgomasters and schepens requested the provincial government for the services of twenty-five negroes to labor eight days at the defensive works, and ordered that one-third of the inhabitants

The Story *of* New Amsterdam

should work at them every third day with a shovel, spade or wheelbarrow. They also approved the mounting of a citizen guard at night and the parade of one company of the town militia daily at five o'clock, each soldier being supplied with a pound of powder and a pound and a half of lead. Finally to insure the proper provisioning of the town, they forbade the brewers to malt hard grain for a period of eight days, or to brew beer at a rate higher than twelve guilders a ton.

The preparations having been made, the magistrates proceeded to petition the governor and council for eight more pieces of cannon, together with the needful appurtenances and ammunition, to be placed upon the walls of Fort Amsterdam. They requested, also, a supply of lead for musket balls, and expressed the opinion that the walls of the town should be defended by the soldiers, the Company's servants and the burgher guard first, lest, if the town itself be captured, the fort become thereby untenable. A favorable response to these petitions was destined to be the last official communication between the director general and council of New

The Passing of New Amsterdam

Netherland and the schout, burgomasters and schepens of New Amsterdam.

The English squadron of four vessels under the command of Colonel Richard Nicolls anchored just below the Narrows, between New Utrecht and Coney Island, on August 29, 1664. Affecting not to know its errand, Stuyvesant sent a commission of four, composed of one councillor, one burgomaster and two clergymen, to inquire the purpose of the visit. On the next day the English commander dispatched in reply four commissioners to demand the surrender "of the town situated on the island and commonly known by the name of Manhattoes." This summons he accompanied with a proclamation assuring protection in person and property to all who would voluntarily submit. As fond as ever of display, the Dutch director general received the English officers with a salvo of artillery that appreciably lessened the scanty stock of powder in the fort. After the communication had been delivered, Stuyvesant called a joint session of the provincial and municipal authorities to consider the matter; but he flatly refused to publish the terms offered lest the people should insist upon immediate surrender. To a meeting of citizens, however, the burgomasters explained the demands of Nicolls. The burghers forthwith called for a copy of Nicolls' proclamation and obtained it despite a flash of the governor's old masterfulness, when he declared that he would not be held responsible for the "calamitous consequences" of submitting to the popular will.

When Nicolls offered still more liberal terms the director general communicated them to the council and burgomasters in the fort, who in turn promptly advised him to make them known to the people, since "all which regarded the public welfare ought to be made public." At first Stuyvesant tried to dissuade the officials from this opinion; then, on finding them inflexible, he burst into a rage and tore Nicolls' letter in pieces. At this news the burghers dropped their work on the fortifications, hurried down to the fort and made a categorical demand for the letter. In vain did Stuyvesant threaten and cajole. Complaints and curses against the Company's misgovernment were mingled with hoarse cries for the letter. To avoid insurrection, the

The Passing of New Amsterdam

director general was forced reluctantly to allow the secretary to piece the fragments together and make out a copy. This he delivered to the burgomasters who in turn read its contents to the people.

Meanwhile Stuyvesant had sent to Nicolls a lengthy statement of the Dutch rights. In response the English officer and his colleagues politely informed him that "they were not come here to dispute about it, but to execute their order and commission without fail either peaceably or by force; and if they had anything to dispute about it, it must be done with his majesty of England, as they could do nothing here in the premises." Nicolls then began to prepare for the bombardment of the fort. Two of the vessels landed troops at Gravesend, who marched up to the Brooklyn shore and effected a junction with colonial volunteers from New England and the Long Island towns. The other ships passed in front of the fort, and anchored between it and Governor's Island with the decks cleared for action and the guns shotted.

Standing at an angle of the fort the sturdy old director general watched the movements of

The Story of New Amsterdam

the enemy while an artilleryman at his side held a lighted fuse ready to apply it at the word of command. The word never came, for just at this moment Domine Megapolensis laid a hand gently on the old soldier's arm. "Of what avail," pleaded the man of God, "are our poor guns against that broadside of more than sixty? It is wrong to shed blood to no purpose." Still confident of ultimate escape, the director general tried to arrange some kind of a compromise with Nicolls. "Tomorrow," said the English commander, "I will speak with you at Manhattan." "Friends," answered Stuyvesant quickly, "will be welcome if they come in a friendly manner." "I shall come with my ships and soldiers," rejoined Nicolls grimly, "and he will be a bold messenger indeed who shall then dare to come on board and solicit terms. . . . Raise the white flag of peace at the fort, and then something may be considered."

Stuyvesant had not yet despaired, though men, women and children implored him to submit. The magistrates, the clergymen and the officers of the burgher guard then adopted a remonstrance depicting the helpless condition of

The Passing of New Amsterdam

the town "encompassed and hemmed in by enemies"; and when the valiant but obstinate old man saw his own son's name in the list he gave way. "Well, let it be so; I would much rather be carried to my grave," was his reply. Thus passed the town of New Amsterdam, thirty-eight years after its first settlement and eleven years after it had been made self-governing.

The question now arises: could New Amsterdam have withstood the English attack? The evidence shows conclusively that the staunch loyalty and all the fighting powers of Stuyvesant were powerless against the overwhelming odds. In the forefront of weakness stood the indifference and procrastination of the burghers and their municipal representatives. A thrift that amounted almost to parsimony, and a phlegmatic temperament that was averse to fighting explain why the town lay exposed to assault. If the walls of Fort Amsterdam succumbed to the snout of the predatory pig they could hardly bear up against English artillery. In fact some of the private houses that clustered about the fort exceeded its walls in height and offered an easy approach by scaling ladders. Though that

The Story of New Amsterdam

stronghold mounted twenty-four guns at the time, with only six hundred pounds of powder available their effectiveness could not have lasted very long. Besides, the hills to the north over which ran the present Broadway commanded the structure completely. Even Stuyvesant himself admitted later that "there was an absolute impossibility of defending the fort, much less the town." As to the ramparts and palisades on Wall Street, the only fortified makeshift the town possessed, they might deter acrobatic Indians from jumping over, but they could not sustain a regular military siege. Furthermore, out of a population then of 1500 perhaps 250 were capable of bearing arms, in addition to the 150 regular soldiers in the fort; and these forces would have had to encounter 1000 English soldiers and sailors as well as a large number of colonial volunteers. Even these defenders could not be relied upon. Neither the burgher guard nor the farmers in the vicinity were inclined to fight, and the troops in the fort, verging on mutiny, muttered about the places "where booty is to be found, and where the young women live who wear gold chains." The inhabitants of

The Passing *of* New Amsterdam

New Amsterdam, naturally, dreaded the consequences of a useless resistance, a capture by storm and the outrageous treatment that would probably follow at the hands of the English colonials "who expected nothing else than pillage, plunder and bloodshed, as men could perceive by their cursing and talking when mention was made of a capitulation."

On September 6 the commission to arrange the terms of surrender met at Stuyvesant's "bouwerie." Among other privileges the Dutch were promised security in property and liberty of conscience. For the present, also, the municipal magistrates should retain their offices and perform their customary duties. Two days later "the fort and town called New Amsterdam upon the island of Manhattoes" formally surrendered. With ex-Director General Stuyvesant at the head, the Dutch garrison marched out "with their arms, drums beating, and colors flying and lighted matches." The fort was renamed Fort James, the city, New York, and the province, the same. All the public rights and franchises, also, of the Dutch West India Company were vested in the Duke of York.

The Story *of* New Amsterdam

In contrast to the sadness with which the masterful old autocrat of New Amsterdam now beheld his army departing for the fatherland, his province passing to the rule of the foreigner and himself destined for the scant solace of retirement, the English gazed with satisfaction at the tight little Dutch town on Manhattan which had now become their own. To quote from contemporary description: "The town is compact and oval, with very fair streets and several good houses . . . built most of brick and stone, and covered with red and black tile . . . after the manner of Holland, to the number of about four hundred . . . which in those parts are held considerable . . . and the land being high, it gives at the distance a pleasing aspect to the spectators. . . . The city has an earthen fort . . . within (which) . . . stand a wind mill and a very high staff upon which a flag is hoisted whenever any vessel is seen in . . . (the lower) bay. The church rises with a lofty doubled roof, between which a square tower looms up. On the one side is the prison, and on the other side of the church is the governor's house. . . . At the waterside stand the gallows and the whip (ping

[188]

VIEW OF NEW YORK, LATE NEW AMSTERDAM, 1670
Arnoldus Montanus, De Nieuwe en Onbekende Weereld,
of Beschrijving van America. Amsterdam, 1671

The Passing *of* New Amsterdam

post) (and) a handsome city tavern adorns the furthest point." Governor Nicolls in fact wrote to the Duke of York that it was "the best of all his majesty's towns in America."

How the burgomasters and schepens of New Amsterdam regarded the change of rule is seen in the communication that they sent to the Dutch West India Company a few days after the surrender. In part it ran as follows: "We, your Honor's loyal, sorrowful, and desolate subjects, cannot neglect nor keep from relating the event which through God's pleasure . . . unexpectedly happened to us in consequence of your Honor's neglect and forgetfulness. . . . Since we have no longer to depend on your Honor's promises of protection, we with all the poor, sorrowing and abandoned commonalty here must fly for refuge to the Almighty . . . not doubting but He will stand by us in this sorely afflicting conjuncture." After the names of the magistrates comes the subscription: "Done at Jorck heretofore named Amsterdam in New Netherland." To the Duke of York they wrote, after Nicolls had administered to them the oath of office: "It has pleased God to bring us under

The Story of New Amsterdam

your Royal Highness' obedience wherein we promise to conduct ourselves as good subjects are bound to do, deeming ourselves fortunate that His Highness has provided us with so gentle, wise and intelligent a gentleman as governor as the Honorable Colonel Nicolls, confident and assured that under the wings of this valiant gentleman we shall bloom and grow like the cedar on Lebanon, especially because we are assured of His Royal Highness' excellent graciousness and care for his subjects and people. . . . Praying then his Royal Highness to be pleased to take our interests and the welfare of this country into serious consideration . . . we are your . . . dutiful subjects, schout, burgomasters and schepens of this town." Just as the previous subscription indicated a state of transition, so now the indorsement of this communication reveals the transition completed: "Done, New Yorck on Manhattans Island, 1664."

Nor did the town fathers forget to honor the man who had guided so long the destinies of New Amsterdam. Says the record: "Petrus Stuyvesant . . . communicates . . . as he is about to depart for Fatherland, that he wishes the bench of burgomasters and schepens every luck and happiness, which was also wished to him by burgomasters and schepens, and that he may settle and arrange his affairs in Fatherland to his satisfaction. And the above named Heer Stuyvesant requests, if the burgomasters and schepens think proper, that they accord to him a certificate of his comportment, which may avail him or his children today or tomorrow. And . . . they resolve as follows: 'We the undersigned schout, burgomasters and schepens of the city of New Yorck on the island of Manathan, formerly named New Amsterdam, certify and declare, at the request of the Honorable Petrus Stuyvesant, late Director General of New Netherland, and who now on the change by the English is about to return to Patria, that his Honor has during about eighteen years administration conducted and demeaned himself not only as [a] Director General according to the best of our knowledge ought to do, on all occurring circumstances, for the interest of the West India Company, but besides as an honest proprietor and patriot of this province and a supporter of the reformed religion.' "

More than a tribute to the sterling character of Stuyvesant, this testimonial was intended to aid him in the defense of his conduct before the Company and the Dutch government. He returned to Manhattan triumphantly vindicated, gave up his house on Whitehall Street to the English governor as an official residence, and retired to his "bouwerie." He and Nicolls, indeed, became fast friends and many were the genial meetings enjoyed by the English officer and his Dutch predecessor at the country house. Ever interested in the civil and religious welfare of his beloved town, the director general lived to the hale old age of eighty, a noble gentleman of the ancient school, and to the day of his death, in 1672, cherishing not a "particle of respect for popular liberty . . . or notions about the rights of man." He was buried in a vault under the little church he had built on his "bouwerie." On the site of that chapel stands the church of "St. Marks-in-the-Bouwerie," and on a stone embedded in the wall of that building the wayfarer may still read the inscription that reveals the last resting-place of Peter Stuyvesant.

Surveying from another angle the circum-

THE LAST RESTING-PLACE OF PETER STUYVESANT
*From a photograph in the possession of
the New York Historical Society*

The Passing of New Amsterdam

stances under which New Amsterdam passed into New York, so as to note the modifications introduced by the English system of government, it may be said that the Dutch magistrates continued to transact their judicial and administrative business for a while as calmly as if nothing unusual had occurred. Not until it became necessary to choose new officers did the first political change appear. Instead of being permitted to present a double number of names from which the governor could select the incumbents for the vacant offices, the retiring board of burgomasters and schepens was allowed merely to nominate the precise number of persons whom the governor then formally appointed. But even this kind of municipal privilege did not last long. In June, 1665, Nicolls abolished the "form of government late in practice within his majesty's town of New York, under the name and style of schout, burgomasters and schepens which are not known or customary in any of his majesty's dominions," and substituted for it "one body politic and corporate under the government of a mayor, aldermen and sheriff." In this arrangement it will be noticed that the office of sheriff is named last, as contrasted with the practice of the Dutch in mentioning that of schout first. The deviation indicates that the English considered the dignity and duties of a sheriff to be inferior to those of the other offices. The Dutch, on the contrary, by making the schout at once sheriff, public prosecutor and supervisor of the customs, assigned him a higher degree of importance, and accordingly placed him at the head of the municipal magistrates. All of the new offices the governor proceeded to fill by direct appointment, his choice for the first mayor of New York falling upon Thomas Willett.

Of the town officials thus designated the mayor, two of the five aldermen and the sheriff were Englishmen. The old burgomasters and schepens, some of whom were on the new board, entered forthwith an earnest protest against the method of appointment, as involving a violation of the terms of surrender, one of which had provided that the magistrates should continue in office until the time of election, and then be allowed to choose their successors as before. To this attempt at a revival of municipal privilege

The Passing *of* New Amsterdam

Nicolls suavely replied that, at the first election held after the establishment of English power, the retiring magistrates had in fact chosen their successors with his approval; and that, since these officials had remained in office up to the present, the terms in question had not suffered infringement. Remonstrate though they might against this close construction of language, the governor's contention was technically correct. His orders from the Duke of York to "establish the government of the city conformable to the customs of England" left him no alternative. He politely ignored the protest, therefore, and on June 24 installed his appointees.

This plan of direct appointment by the governor, instead of the Dutch method of proposal by the town officials themselves, remained in force until 1669 when, after Nicolls had been succeeded by Colonel Francis Lovelace, the mayor and aldermen prevailed on the new governor to restore the Dutch practice. They accordingly submitted to him a list of names, double the number required for the offices of mayor, aldermen and sheriff, out of which Lovelace graciously chose the necessary half. On the occasion, also, of his accession to the governorship Lovelace presented to the town authorities on behalf of the Duke of York what was called at the time "the gayety and circumstantial part of government," namely, a new seal, a silver mace, and seven ornate gowns for the seven dignitaries of New York.

Other modifications introduced into New Amsterdam by the advent of English rule were: the employment of the jury system as against the Dutch method of referees; the support of clergymen by the town instead of by the provincial government; and in 1668 the abolition of the exclusive burgher right created eleven years before. The explanation of the act last mentioned lay in the fact that subjection to English jurisdiction had removed the fear of competition from colonial neighbors, and that the municipal offices had ceased to be the prerogative of great burghers alone.

Over a further modification in local practice quite a little controversy arose. This had to do with a proposition to quarter soldiers on the inhabitants. According to Governor Nicolls, the soldiers of the garrison at Fort James "were not boarded or washed nor had pot or kettle to cook for themselves," and were inclined withal to insolence and disturbance as a result of such conditions. For the sake of the public peace he believed it needful to quarter the soldiers on the citizens. To this end the provincial government was to furnish a certain amount of provisions, and the householder concerned to receive from the town two guilders a week. To enable the municipality to meet the expenditure, he would reassign it the income from the excise, the weigh-scales and the ferry, all of which had been seized by the provincial government at the time of the surrender. Out of the fifty householders, however, summoned to consider the question, only ten professed willingness to harbor the soldiers. That the rate of board, rather than the principle of the quartering of troops in this form, had something to do with the reluctance was manifest, when in October, 1665, the governor agreed to increase the payments to be made to the temporary landlord, for board, lodging, washing, small beer and firewood. When this was done the objections disappeared.

However well the English soldiers may have

The Story *of* New Amsterdam

been treated at the hands of the New York householders, they could not cope with the great fleet of twenty-three Dutch warships, having on board 1600 men under the command of Admirals Evertsen and Binckes, when it arrived off Sandy Hook, August 7, 1673. English commissioners were sent to demand why the Dutch fleet had come in "such a hostile manner to disturb his majesty's subjects in this place." To this demand the Dutch commanders replied that they had come simply to take what was "their own and their own they would have." After further negotiations, at the expiration of a specified half hour the Dutch vessels opened fire on the fort, killing several of the garrison, and wounding others. Captain Anthony Colve, also, landed with six hundred men on the shore of the Hudson back of the present Trinity Church and marched down Broadway; but, before they could arrive at the fort they were met with proposals for surrender on substantially the same terms as those of 1664. The naval commanders now assumed possession of the province in the name of the Dutch government, and proceeded to rechristen the province New Netherland, its

SIGNATURES OF DUTCH GOVERNORS—PETER MINUIT,
WOUTER VAN TWILLER, WILLIAM KIEFT,
PETER STUYVESANT AND ANTHONY COLVE

The Passing *of* New Amsterdam

capital, New Orange, instead of New Amsterdam, and the fort, after the name of the stadholder of the Netherlands who later became King William III of England, William Henry. Captain Colve they appointed military governor.

On August 15 a general meeting of the citizens who had cordially welcomed the restoration of Dutch rule was convened at the town hall to elect six persons for burgomasters and fifteen for schepens from among the wealthy people and those professing the Reformed Calvinistic faith only. From this number the military government selected three names for burgomasters, thus making one additional, and the usual number of five schepens. The schout as the most important officer was appointed directly, and the new municipal régime inaugurated on August 17.

But if the people of New Orange, formerly New Amsterdam and New York, imagined that the return of Dutch rule meant a restoration of municipal privilege, the military governor soon convinced them of their mistake. Indeed the system of control now to be exercised by the provincial authorities was more severe than any-

The Story of New Amsterdam

thing the town had known for twenty years. Viewed in the light of the conduct displayed by the inhabitants of New Amsterdam on the advent of the English in 1664, the strictness of the military government seems due, less to a fear of reconquest from that quarter than to a suspicion that the political affections cherished by the citizens of Manhattan were a trifle inconstant. Of course the municipal magistrates had to renounce the insignia of English forms—"the gayety and circumstantial part of government"—furnished by the official seal, mace and gowns, which were carefully deposited in the fort. Governor Colve, furthermore, restricted the nomination of the double number of persons by the retiring board to the "most wealthy . . . and such . . . as are of the Reformed Christian religion, or at least well affected towards it," reserved the right to keep the present incumbents in office, and ordered a military commissioner to preside at the sessions of the magistracy in his behalf. Naturally the schout, burgomasters and schepens resented the suspicion involved in the presence of this officer, and protested to the governor that it violated the practices of the fatherland, injured the privileges of the bench and the burghership, and seriously depreciated their standing in the community. But the stern threat of instant dismissal from office checked any further remonstrance, and in July, 1674, much to their disgust, the burgomasters and schepens beheld their especial aversion, the military commissioner, elevated to the permanent presidency of the board in the capacity of schout. In the following month, also, the governor tightened the reins of control by reducing the number of burgomasters from three to two and the number of schepens from five to three, while he retained the direct appointment of the schout. He did allow the old system of double election for the burgomasters and schepens to continue, but modified it by having only one burgomaster retire at a time, thus insuring the possibility of a longer term of service if deemed necessary.

Just as the governor believed it advisable to forestall any refractory conduct on the part of the town magistrates, so did these officials in turn deem it necessary to check the disorderly practices on Sunday, which the recent changes had probably aggravated. The last ordinance on the observance of the Sabbath to be framed under Dutch auspices on Manhattan closely resembled the earlier regulations on the subject. It forbade "from sunrise to sundown . . . all sorts of handicraft, trade and traffic, gaming, boat racing, or running with carts or wagons, fishing, fowling, running and picking nuts, strawberries and the like, all riotous racing, calling and shouting of children in the streets, together with all unlawful exercises and games, drunkenness, frequenting taverns or tap-houses, dancing, card-playing, ball-playing, rolling nine-pins or bowls . . . which is more in vogue on this than on any other day." All tavern-keepers and tapsters, therefore, were "strictly enjoined to entertain no clubs on this day . . . nor . . . suffer any games in their houses or places," under a heavy penalty. And if any children were caught on the street, playing, running or shouting "previous to the termination of the last preaching, the officers of the law may take their hat or upper garment, which shall not be restored to their parents until they have paid a fine." The intent of such prohibition was "not that a stranger or citizen shall not buy a drink of wine or beer for the assuaging of his thirst, but only to prevent the sitting of clubs on the Sabbath, whereby many are hindered (from) resorting to Divine Worship." Taken as a whole the ordinance indicates clearly two facts: first, that the earlier enactments against the sale of liquor on the Sabbath had undergone some modification, and second, that, judging from the list of offences catalogued, Manhattan must have been a lively island for young and old, notions about the ponderous solemnity of Dutchmen to the contrary notwithstanding.

About this time also it appears that the fences, as well as the morals, of the people residing between New Haarlem and the "Fresh Water" in particular were in need of correction. In the instructions drawn up by the magistrates for the fence-viewers it is stated that, not only should an individual keep his own fence in repair, but that, if he thought his neighbor's fences not "good or sufficient . . . and dreading damage thereby" from migratory animals, he should first request his neighbor "in love and friendship to repair his fence," otherwise he was to complain to the proper officials. Also, the depredations still committed upon the fortifications by the burrowing snouts of peregrine pigs led the military governor to command that their sphere of activity "within this city and its jurisdiction unto the Fresh Water" be confined within fences on pain of confiscation.

In order to place the town in a proper state of defence against the risk of English hostility, the governor ordered the removal of all houses near the fort, thus safeguarding the structure against one point of attack at least. For their losses the owners received compensation in money or in land. The people of New Orange, furthermore, had to perform military service, part of which consisted in working on the fortifications; otherwise they had to pay a special tax. So as to facilitate the performance of the financial duties of the town in this respect, the revenues from the excise, the weigh-scales and the ferry, which the provincial government had seized at the beginning of the Dutch reoccupation, were again turned over to it.

With the same general object in view, Colve issued a series of military regulations. He for-

The Passing *of* New Amsterdam

bade the inhabitants of New Orange to export provisions, and commanded them to lay in a stock that would last eight months. Since the fortifications had nearly attained completion, a corresponding strictness had to be observed in the duties of the civil and military authorities. Not only could no one enter or leave the town except by the regular gates, but an elaborate formality had to be maintained in guarding these portals. At drumbeat, a half hour before sundown, the militia paraded in front of the town hall. Then the burgomasters received the municipal keys from the guard at the fort, and, with an escort of six, proceeded in state to lock the gates, and assign the citizen night-watch. By a similar pageant at sunrise the gates were opened and the keys restored to their keepers at the fort.

For the domestic habits of the burghers this martial service must have been rather unpleasant, and the honor an irksome one to the burgomasters, especially on cold winter mornings. The pageant in which the magistrates took part has been thus described, with some words of eulogy on the burghers and their town:

The Story *of* New Amsterdam

"Lo! with the sun came forth a goodly train,
The portly mayor with his full guard of state.
Hath aught of evil vexed their fair domain
That thus its limits they perambulate
With heavy measured steps and brows of care,
Counting its scattered roofs with fixed portentous stare?
Behold the keys, with solemn pomp restored
To one in warlike costume stoutly braced—
He of yon fort the undisputed lord—
Deep lines of thought are on his forehead traced,
As though of Babylon, the proud command,
Or hundred-gated Thebes were yielded to his hand.
See here and there the buildings cluster round,
All to the street their cumbrous gables stretching,
With square-clipped trees and snug enclosures bound—
A most uncouth material for sketching—
Each with its stoop from whose sequestered shade
The Dutchman's evening pipe in cloudy volumes played.
Yet deem them not for ridicule a theme—
These worthy burghers with their spouses kind—

The Passing *of* New Amsterdam

Scorning of heartless pomp the gilded dream
To deeds of peaceful industry inclined;
In hospitality sincere and grave,
Inflexible in truth, in simple virtue brave.
Hail! mighty city—high must be his fame
Who round thy bounds at sunrise now should walk—
Still wert thou lovely, whatsoe'er thy name—
New Amsterdam, New Orange, or New York,
Whether in cradle sleep on seaweed laid,
Or on thine island throne in queenly power arrayed."

But the days of New Orange were numbered. At the conclusion of peace between England and the Netherlands, early in 1674, New Netherland reverted to the former country and again became New York. The entry in the municipal records announcing the fact runs as follows: "The governor general appearing in court (of schout, burgomasters and schepens) states that he has now received . . . absolute orders from . . . their High Mightinesses for the restitution of this province . . . to his majesty of Great Britain pursuant to the treaty of peace . . .

with further orders that he return home with the garrison as soon as possible, which his Honor resolved to communicate to the court, informing them . . . that, if they had yet any representation to make to their High Mightinesses, it would be willingly presented by his Honor." Since the recent military régime had apparently moderated an earlier enthusiasm for the fatherland, the magistrates answered simply: "The worshipful court hath thanked the governor." Finally, it is stated that "on the tenth of November, anno 1674, the province of New Netherland is surrendered by Governor Colve to Governor Major Edmund Andros in behalf of his majesty of Great Britain." Thus did New Orange pass from view and with it the days of the Dutch dominion.

Though New York grew up as an English town and became the metropolis of the American nation, it has remained true to the memory of its Dutch forerunner, for when we would personify the city we call it "Father Knickerbocker." Perchance the spirit of Peter Stuyvesant yet stumps along unseen amid the multitudes and guards with jealous care his "island of the hills"!

A NOTE ON THE TYPE IN
WHICH THIS BOOK IS SET

This book is set on the Linotype in Garamond, a modern rendering of the type first cut in the sixteenth century by Claude Garamond (1510–1561). He was a pupil of Geofroy Tory and is believed to have based his letters on the Venetian models although he introduced a number of important differences, and it is to him we owe the letter which we know as Old Style. He gave to his letters a certain elegance and a feeling of movement which won for their creator an immediate reputation and the patronage of the French King, Francis I.